THE HIDDEN WORLD

Volume 6

THE ELDER WORLD
THE LORELEI
BEYOND THE VERGE
& MORE!

The Shaver Mystery

Global Communications

THE HIDDEN WORLD
Volume 6
THE SHAVER MYSTERY

Richard S. Shaver
Ray Palmer
Dewitt C. Chipman
Dennis Crenshaw

This revised edition and new cover art
Copyright © 2009
Timothy Green Beckley
DBA Global Communications, All Rights Reserved

EAN: 978-1-60611-070-6
ISBN: 1-60611-070-5

Originally Published by Palmer Publications, Summer 1962 A-6

No part of this book may be reproduced, stored in retrieval system or transmitted in any form or by any means, electronic, mechanical, photocopying, recording, without express permission of the publisher.

Timothy Green Beckley: Editorial
Director Carol Rodriguez: Publishers
Assistant Sean Casteel: Associate Editor
William Kern: Editorial Assistant
Cover Art: Tim Swartz

Printed in the United States of
America For free catalog write:
Global Communications
P.O. Box 753
New Brunswick, NJ 08903

Free Subscription to Conspiracy Journal E-Mail
Newsletter www.conspiracyjournal.com

Note: Each Page contains two sets of page numbers. The first set corresponds to total page number in the entire series. The page number below that shows the page number for this book only

The HIDDEN WORLD

ISSUE NO. A-6
SUMMER, 1962

Contents

The Vindication of
   Richard S. Shaver.........iv
  Dennis Crenshaw

EDITORIAL 958
  Ray Palmer

THE ELDER WORLD 964
  Richard S. Shaver

THE LORELEI 978
  Richard S. Shaver

BEYOND THE VERGE ... 993
  DeWitt C. Chipman

LETTERS 1135
  From The Readers

Cover Paintings by
Myrtle Ruth Duke

Global Communications

The Vindication of Richard S. Shaver

By Dennis Crenshaw
Editor: The Hollow Earth Insider

When the Editor of Hidden World asked me to do a short article to be used as a forward for this issue my first thought was that over the years I had written almost everything I knew about Mr. Shaver. Then I remembered a news report I'd read on the internet just a few weeks ago that had brought the name Richard Shaver screaming to the front of my thoughts. That report reiterated the fact that as time goes on I realize more and more that Richard S. Shaver was indeed a man ahead of his time. I can offer an easy example of proof of that statement that would stop any argument against that fact with one glance. On the cover of Volume 1 of this Hidden World series is a drawing of a Dero as seen by Mr. Shaver. The illustration consists of a Dero setting comfortable in his leisure chair deep down in his underground lair watching the goings and comings of humans on the surface. He is watching them remotely over a computer screen. At his fingertips is a keyboard. I agree there are knobs on the keyboard instead of lettered keys. But no one can deny it is a computer. And this illustration was first published in 1943.

THE HIDDEN WORLD

Television was still around the corner and computers were a gleam in several young inventors' brains. Then there is that amazing news report I read the other day.

I recently had the privilege of working with Mary Martin (The Best of the Hollow Earth Hassle – Global Communications 2008) on a project to release a lost Richard Shaver interview she, Tom LeVesque and Richard Shaver had participated in on the Hilly Rose show back in 1972. I think this was probably his last live interview. While converting this amazing cassette tape to CD I realized something that has sort of been brushed aside when it comes to talk of the strange world of Richard S. Shaver. The Shaver Mystery overshadows another remarkable discovery by this extraordinary man. In fact in his last years he had put the Shaver Mystery and the hidden World aside. As he stated in the interview, he had grown tired of talking about the Shaver Mystery because he had grown tired of people not believing him and calling him a liar and a "nut". Then he began to talk passionately of the work that he was doing at the present time (1972). Work that he would actually be involved in for the rest of his life. Work that made many people in the scientific community roll their eyes at the thought of it.

He had moved to Summit Arkansas and opened a small "Rock Shop" behind his humble dwelling. But he wasn't just selling rocks. As he explained to Hilly and his radio audience in the interview:

Excerpts:

"Dot [Richard's wife] brought in these rocks and put them on my desk. They set there for quite awhile. Then [one day] I really looked at the things and said, "Here's what I've been looking for."

Shaver goes on to report that he started to slice these rocks into slabs and he stated that he begin to realize that these were not just rocks but that they contained messages from the ancients. He further states that "What they are, are huge libraries of picture rocks and they are very common, very valuable and very easy to see."

Although Ray Palmer does devote part 2 of the rare hard-to-find 1975 book *"The Secret World -Volume 1: "Pictures in Stone""* to Richard Shaver's discovery of picture rocks not much has been said about this phase of this far-seeing man's life since. I guess the ever-lasting interest in the doings of the Dero and Tero and the whole Shaver Mystery has had more than a little to do with scant attention being paid to, - or realization of - the true significance of the other Shaver discovery, his picture rocks and his claim that they contained the library of an ancient civilization.

So you can imagine my surprise and delight when I ran across the

THE HIDDEN WORLD

following report at ireport.com

An unknown language consisting of visual communications has been deciphered from certain small stones called "Petro Photoglyphs". The collection or library of these artifacts was discovered as surface samples in 1994 near the Missouri and Kentucky border. The 'Petro Photoglyphs' project hologram images in photographic detail when properly illuminated. Stone objects that provide time capsule communications as they require our modern technologies to view and our data base of current human knowledge and understanding to decipher them. Scribed by a highly advanced inscription technology these objects provide proof that an ancient and currently unknown intelligence is attempting to contact us via a collection of stone etched 'DVDs'. Pictured are two artifacts with a variety of the captured visual projections: The Genesis Petroglyph (right) and The Unicorn Petroglyph (left). A record of detailed photographic images from the dawn of human understanding and proof of contact with a highly advanced and unknown intelligence. A unique website dedicated to research with petro photoglyphic artifacts: www.impactoptics.com

The above article with a slide show of photos can be seen at:
http://www.ireport.com/docs/DOC-302153

As I said at the beginning of this piece . . . As time goes on I realize that, say what you may, Richard S. Shaver was a far-seeing man. Mr. Shaver you are vindicated.

This brings us back to this series, the Hidden World. Maybe it's time Richard Shaver's hidden world was given a bit more scrutiny. After all he knew a computer was down the road. He located an ancient library and saw historical photos long before anyone in the scientific community would even consider such a thing. And it was all right at their feet. All they had to do was pick up a rock. That's what Shaver did. Maybe its time to look a little further under our feet. After all . . . Shaver did.

Contact Dennis Crenshaw at: denniscrenshaw@gmail.com

Editor; www.thehollowearthinsider.com

THE HIDDEN WORLD
SACRED FLOWER SYMBOLS OF ANCIENT LEMURIA

The Sunken Continent
In The Pacific

WORTINERIA

EDITORIAL

By Ray Palmer

THE PLANS OF MICE AND MEN often go astray. In the case of THE HIDDEN WORLD, we believe it can be expected that plans will go astray. Thus it is that this Summer issue of THE HIDDEN WORLD is just going to press on September 6. Summer is almost a memory. However, since the Fall issue will be on time, and will follow this one by only a few weeks, it would seem that we have come out even in the end. We apologize to our readers who had to wait so long for the sixth issue; but at the same time let us take this opportunity to remind you that it is quite likely that this magazine may appear on a rather indefinite schedule, but there will be four issues per year without fail, and you need not write and ask for your issue unless you have seen a copy on the newsstands, and haven't received yours. In that case, Uncle Sam has definitely skipped your mailbox, and we will send you another.

Among the plans that went astray was the plan we had for the contents of this issue. It was certainly not what eventually found its way into the magazine. So, instead of the unusual Indian history of 10,000 years ago, when the Grand Canyon was formed overnight, we present a novel by DeWitt C. Chipman called Beyond The Verge. This is but one of many mysterious books relating a history of a hollow earth, and in this one we find perhaps the most surprising account of all, because of the way it agrees with so much of the evidence that has come forth from the Shaver Mystery, and from the many other sources in our lifetime of research into the Hidden World. You will find that many puzzling questions are answered by this book, but at the same time many more are raised. We have future answers for some of them, but for others we remain as baffled as you will be. Yet, in presenting this novel, we are adding one more facet to the entire story of The Hidden World that we are giving you. It is a vital part of the tremendous whole that we hope to give you before this series of magazines comes to an end. We have only begun to give you the whole story, and for those of you who missed the first 5 issues of THE HIDDEN WORLD, and who are particularly interested, we must advise you that it would be an excellent idea to order back issues now. They will not last forever, and already the back stock is quite out of balance, and some issues will be sold out before others, and complete sets will be impossible.

In this issue we present one more bit of that great novel Richard S. Shaver began writing and never completed, nor even marshalled into form. This fragment might be said to have been the beginning of his novel, and it bears the title of the book as Shaver intended it - "The Elder World". You will find it a fascinating bit of writing, and a revealing one.

Another bit of the novel is a chapter that was titled "The Lorelei", and we have retained that title. Its place in the novel was never indicated, and today it remains as a sort of detached and floating fragment, almost aimless in its design. Yet it contains a great deal of the lore of the Shaver Mystery. The Lorelei were those maidens who graced the legends of the ancient Greeks, and also were the awe and terror of the inhabitants of the world of that day. Today, says Shaver, the real meaning of the Lorelei has been lost; and in this fragment he gives us the lie of the lore of the past. Yes, there was a great wisdom in those days, a lore that is now forgotten, and what is not forgotten has been turned into a lie. Perhaps some of it is restored in this bit of novel, this unrelated chapter in a planned work that never took definite form. Perhaps it is better this way. To place all the material presented in THE HIDDEN WORLD, even that portion of it known as The Shaver Mystery, into a category, would have been impossible. As presented here, it is for the reader to place into the puzzle as a single piece of a rather indeterminate color and shape.

Here lies the fascination of looking into the dim reaches of the Hidden World. What we glimpse so fleetingly can many times suddenly flash forth in our mind's eye as a complete facet of a jewel we had not suspected before. Or it can bring to reality and understanding a mystery that has plagued us for years, and whose very nature we did not comprehend until all at once we find the lie in the ancient lore, and the truth stands forth nakedly before us, sometimes beautiful, and sometimes horrible.

Much of the past was beautiful. Some of it was utter terror. But we have a heritage from that past that is vital and alive today, and whether it ends for us in beauty or disaster is a question we must answer by finding out the truth. The Hidden World must be exposed. We must understand it. We must know its beginnings, its present status, and its future plans for us. We must shake its shackles from us and live our lives in the freedom to which we are entitled.

As you read this issue, you will find a strange mixture of mystery both proposed and explained. You will find the legends of ancient Greece, the Old Testament (particularly Genesis and Exodus) and the Shaver Mystery all mixed up with the theory of a hollow earth. But you will find that it is not at all the hodge-podge that you might believe it must be. Instead you will find a picture beginning to unfold, and you will be interested in what is to come - for in the material on hand, there is a single great picture that will emerge that you will need to take bit by bit as your editor has over the years or you will not grasp it. It is important that you do not form previous opinions, but merely assimilate everything that is presented, and watch for the links that will forge it into one chain of evidence that will convince you of the reality of everything that you have read. Don't accept anything without this certain conviction that has to come only with much thought, study and analysis of the individual bits of the whole.

The greatest difficulty will come in "unlearning" what you had previously believed to be knowledge. It is the lie of the lore that you must discover. It is a sad truth that much of what we "know" is not knowledge, but a falsehood that has been foisted upon us in order to steal from us our birthright. Our coat of many colors, that heritage of Esau, is a camouflage that has been draped over us, blinding us to reality, and guiding us toward a fatal and deadly destiny that we must avoid by discovering the true nature of this world we live in. It is significant that the Bible says "In those days there were giants in the Earth". It is significant that we say we live in the world. It is a lie of the lore that we live ON the world. We must know for a certainty just where it is that we live, where our ancestors lived, and where our descendents will live. It is important that we know whether we ourselves will live, even after we die, and if we do, where that living place will be. Not only is the world "hidden" around us, there are hidden worlds unsuspected by us, yet vital to us, because from them come those "directives" which have made blind slaves of us.

On the cover this month you will find a title "In Those Days There Were Giants In The Earth". We had intended to cover that subject in this issue, but it was one of the casualties of the many difficulties that beset us in getting it out. However, we will include it in a future issue. What is interesting about this cover (both front and back) is that we printed it several months ago, and we selected the two flower designs because herein lies one of the fascinating facets of the Shaver Mystery. Shaver wrote a story once from one of his "thought records", in which he described the ancient noble houses of Mu, and gave the names of the nobles. They were very long names, and hard to pronounce, so we shortened them. Yet, at the same time we received a series of colored drawings of flowers and crests of the royal houses of ancient Mu from a person who called herself Myrtle Ruth Duke. The fascinating thing was that she titled her drawings with precisely the same long and complicated names Shaver had used in his story. Myrtle Ruth Duke had received her drawings by psychic impression from spirits of the Lemurians, via the occult. Shaver got his from "thought records" played back to him mentally from the caves. We can argue for many days on which was which, but the fact is, the names were identical.

When we finally wrote Myrtle Ruth Duke, our letter was returned, saying "unknown at this address". Through the years we tried to locate her. No luck.

Now listen to this. We decided to print some of her drawings in the hope she would see them and write us. But those drawings were still in our printing plant (and are at the moment of this writing) yet we received a letter from her, saying she had suddenly felt "impelled" to write us, and that it was important. In this letter she said Myrtle Ruth Duke was not her real name, and thus our failure to find her, plus the fact she had moved from the original address, and naturally had not left a forwarding address for her pen name. We have not had time to reply to her letter, but we certainly will - for here is another instance of those weird happenings that seem to accompany the Shaver Mystery; more evidence of that "hidden world" that acts so mysteriously in our daily lives.

We want to call your attention to the letters printed in this issue of THE HIDDEN WORLD. They are not old letters, but recent letters, detailing events that have just happened. They are the same events that created so much excitement when the Shaver Mystery first begain. They prove that the Mystery is not dead, but still goes on, and in even greater force today. Today hundreds of thousands, if not millions, of people are hearing voices. They are hearing voices that say the SAME thing to people who have never been, nor ever will be associated. They say things that fall into a pattern that is very significant, and often frightening. Yet we must not be frightened, but we must seek to understand. For it is very important that we realize that people who hear voices are not insane. True there are cases of illness and injury in which the result is hallucinatory voices in the mind which are not really there. But psychiatrists are either unaware of the fact that real voices speak to people, or they do not speak about it because it is a thing they cannot explain. What an expert cannot explain, he ignores or denies, because to admit he cannot explain it is to admit that he is not an expert. This editor knows that voices are real. He knows it from many many thousands of reports from people who tell him what the voices say. It is not insanity when voices speak to thousands and say IDENTICAL things. It is a voice capable of reaching many minds, by some mysterious means, and enforcing its propaganda upon them. It is a voice that has a positive physical source, and it is not in the mind of a paranoid. It would be inconceivable that two persons, much less thousands, could go insane and hear a voice in their minds saying idenical words, words that have a definite purpose, such as a POLITICAL purpose! If you say otherwise, you are not insane, you are illogical and possibly even stupid. Reasoning is a power given to us all, but used by very few of us. Some of can be hit over the head with a baseball bat, and still deny that there is such a thing as a baseball game.

Thus it is, in the letters presented this issue, and there are only a few, unfortunately, due to the changes in our plans, that we find an astounding pattern. It will puzzle you enormously. Perhaps it will ring a bell in your mind, and you will say - that has happened to me too! If this is true, please write and tell us about it. No need to sign your name, if it may embarrass you, or cause you trouble. It is the information that is important. And you cannot fabricate a lie and make it fit into the pattern. (It would surprise you to know how many persons try to do this, possibly as an attempt to ridicule us, or to play a joke on us, or out of sheer stupidity. But none of these letters find their way into anything but the wastebasket, because these letter writers do not even suspect the lie of the lore, and they fall into the trap of repeating the lie, and thus remaining outside the pattern.) - Rap.

THE ELDER WORLD

By RICHARD S. SHAVER

TO GET STARTED, I want to dedicate the book to woman. Not a woman, but to the inner difference that makes woman what she is to men.

To that magnetic magic of sex that is above and beyond thought; to the strange mystery of energy that gives birth through dual forms of male and female; to the mystery behind the chiefest attraction of our life; to what we really mean when we say woman - I dedicate this work.

She, the mother of the thought of life-birth. The kiss of the morning to her, to the scent of growth and fire of the light that is coming to make our world bright again as it was when it was young.

She promised us life when she bore us - and she will in time fulfill that promise. As yet in my "life" she has not done so.

There are certain things to which we do not dedicate this book. There are some who expect us to go on about how the angels may flit and the Gods prance the hill-tops once again, how the fallen may rise and the buried be dug up - how the dead may live again. They can stop here.

964

How the ancient magic may live once again, yes. But this is not fiction or fantasy - it is as sober a job as we could manage against terrific obstacles.

Oh, I wonder, right enough, about how we artists and fantasists seem appointed to clutter up the minds of men with symbols of decay. How very strong seems the obligation to go on about the outworn folly of madmen, the symbols of degeneration, the clutter of idiocy called alchemy, esoteric secrets, grammarie and what-not. Those who expect any such performance can stop reading here, too.

I often wonder how it is so many writers expect to hold an audience with the odor that arises from long continued preoccupation with the grave, with the impossible life-in-death of the ghoul, with the more "weird" fantasies. What are they about? Why this steady and repetitive emphasis on the symbols of death? Is death, then, a friend?

We want this book to be a path along which the faint, far screamings from the past-night may become a terrible shouting in the wind that will blast all men into a seeing never before theirs.

But to you who expect of Shaver some wool about how the corrupted bones of corpses may prance into life, or the terrifying sight of some dread-eyed hunk of long dead meat may give an effluvium of terror to some thrill-starved escapist - away with the silly stuff.

This book is not fantasy or weirdisms, not fiction or adventure. It is sober work.

I deplore the past necessity of describing skinny witches debauching themselves with Satan's over-ripe lustiness; deplore the fatal charm of the concept of some "risen" spirit of evil which has given rise to so many untruthful hours of writing; deplore the whole trend of thought in fantasy and science-fiction. I want to change it. But this book has little to do with all that, and those of my following who expect any such shenanigans are going to be disappointed - especially so if they do not read and see exactly what I do want to say to them.

We do not want in these pages any such foolishness as parades through all modern escapist's literary dreams. No

965

matter how instant the effect of a decayed hand upon the neck, we cannot in the interests of sober truth have it mean anything but silly death, unnecessary evil and un-needed wool.

Now, knowing this book is not fiction and not fantasy, not science-fiction or weirdism, we will leave it up to you to decide for yourself what it really may be.

Please don't expect too much and your reward may be great.

To me, writing a book should be something a man does because he knows people need his work terribly, rather than something he does in the spirit of a carny barker: to lure marks into a sideshow where terrific nonsense will seem credible.

It should be something a man does bravely, showing his hand openly, betting his all upon its acceptance and upon the understanding and the gentle careful thought of the reader. I deplore the usual mountebank approach to writing, the desire to fool the public into accepting a simulacrum as the real thing. I think that all modern literature has fallen into a seedy kind of rut where writers think that writing is a business of word-sharping, a kind of depraved sleight of hand which does not ever fully confess its dishonesty. I deplore the results upon the minds of all men; work which should develop them into greater men makes instead more wool-headed idiots than before - begging your pardon.

I deplore the whole target of modern thought: if you can detect a goal before the efforts of the usual word-monger, I defy you to present it and to prove that it exists.

So, taking out a literary license of the broadest kind, and craving your indulgence for my shortcomings and the necessary incompleteness of my data, I give you a book called the "Elder World".

THE ELDER RACE

FOR SIXTEEN YEARS, I have known that there was an Elder Race. For three years and more I have been selling fiction based on my knowledge of their existence in the far past.

THE HIDDEN WORLD

For quite as long I have writhed with frustration that my purpose in writing - to save some of the mighty knowledge left us from the past - was not generally understood. Few seemed to have the necessary penetration to sense how inescapably true, how mighty and vast and necessary beyond life these "fictional" stories were to men.

So I work on this book, none of which is fiction (but for a few skits to give an atmosphere I have no other means to convey) and in it I shall display all the notes and scribbling and telaug conversations of many years. All that I know about the mighty race must be explained in every possible way, so that even the least deductive mind cannot escape the overwhelming evidence. Some day, some student worthy of the title "student" will realize that still hidden under the rocks of mother Earth DOES lie the terrifying immensity of the wisdom of a God-like race that once made their home on earth. Or rather, in the earth - or are their works left extant only far below the surface because the earth's surface was scoured clean by sun flames? Their records indicate the latter.

Readers of the modern scientific fiction type of tale are accustomed to stories of "superior" races on "alien" planets, to descriptions of the extreme complexity of an alien and superior science and a civilization with endless centuries of "scientific" development. Yet when I presented what I know to be the real thing to them, they (or rather the thickheaded minority of them) responded with a campaign to excommunicate me for imposing upon their "intelligence". Needless to say I was very disappointed to discover the audience had been inoculated against the virus of truth by an anti-body injected into them over many years. They preferred their fiction - quite a few of them.

The real thing inevitably carried with it the truth of long term degeneration for the race of man - which I find unacceptable to the optimistic school of idealism as spread in our modern pedagogical centers of learning.

Sorry as I am to disrupt the neat edifice of "this is the best of all possible worlds" school of thought, I have to insist it is much better to diagnose what sickness afflicts mankind than to wrap their ailing minds in the many layers of shock absorbent wool with which the present day mind is preserved from exposure to the ancient truths of life on earth.

We live on the down beat of a long-term slide from a peak of accomplishment almost impossible for our latter day minds to envision. Even to consider the manner of life of the Elder Race is for a modern, virtuous, moral mind an infinite adventure in wishful sinning.

However, to see the truth we have to look at it - and the Elder Race were so vital and virile they did indulge in what to us seems shockingly sensual pastimes and pursuits.

But just how a modern man would behave if he were chock full of hormones, testosterones, vitamins and every other stimulant to vital healthy living which a science ages old could give him - the modern man would be arrested for thinking, I suppose.

So, like Christ, I forgive those enemies who call my serious efforts to portray what is beyond the modern mind even to understand, I forgive those who have called Shaver "smutty" "oversexed" and various other epithets - and at them all I throw this book, knowing they will decry my every effort to be entertaining as "salacious". I have no doubt they will find many a target for their darts, being what they are, the modern philistines. So, if this be sin, why, make the most of it; if this be evil, then evil must be a strange way of life indeed. Perhaps it might be better to know something about it; you might stumble into some.

My stories of the Elder race have aroused almost every kind of reaction except the one I wanted. What I wanted was a practical reaction, from men with strong minds and plenty of resources to back a real effort to get to the bottom of the cavern secrecy and get out of the caverns whatever they contain of value for modern surface man's science and industry. Several thousand such people have organized into a "Shaver Mystery Club" for this purpose, but of resources and monumental efforts toward the goal we have yet to attain the optimum.

Others reacted exactly as I hoped they would not: they

THE HIDDEN WORLD

set off on cavern explorations unprepared for what dangers there are undeniably to be faced. Some of these were wiped out, for the secrecy they employed made the wiping out of the members a quite confidential affair so that only whispers of their fate have leaked out. I want right here to point out that if there is reason for such expeditions, there is vastly greater reason for efficient publicity about it before it starts - for then they will be quite safe as their sudden demise would expose the agent of their destruction. This is very important, and I want to emphasize it strongly.

Now, to get back to Elder life, the scale was gigantic. It is best understood by taking a careful look at the photo (published elsewhere in this book) of a "granite outcrop" in India's Hyderabad, and visualizing the tremendous group sculpture it undoubtedly once was. There is also the picture of Devil's Tower, Sundance Wyoming, to give you an idea of how trees grew in the days when Ygdrasil was no legend. There is no particular reason for assuming that Devil's Tower is not a stump petrified, except that it is so very big. But there was a period of giganticism on earth, and life did not die off every few years, but kept right on growing, for the conditions were very different.

The men who flourished when that vast stone tower was a tree in leaf were also big beyond belief. (This is of course quite ridiculous; you are to drop this book and pick up some religious tract and indulge your credulity in ordinary angels and omniscience watching over you - or perhaps some technical dissertation on how Einstein discovered that space was curved because of the crumples in the continuum.)

Nevertheless and in spite of general incredulity as to all things legendary, the giant race of the legends did exist and were wiped out by those catastrophes which reduced the size of earth's trees to their present day dwarfage.

Whether "the big race" (as they are called by modern cavern dwellers to distinguish them from latter races) who peopled the caves, bored their caverns before such trees grew under the first primeval sun, or whether that tree grew before or after they were here on earth - we will probably never know. But there is a vast amount we can know about

969

them. Though it is much mixed with latter cavern races, it is usually easily distinguished.

We do not even know if there was a moon overhead when that tree grew. Some scientists hold forth lengthily on the time of the moon's capture by the earth, and date the floods of legendary times over all earth from that capture, due to its influence on our gravity as it took up its first un-circular erratic orbit. (Erractic at that time, you sticklers for exactitudes.)

I HAVE SEEN THE CAVERNS, and the work of that vast inhuman humanity who built the homes of the caverns, and I am content. I know that this life we call "life" is but a faint reflection of a mighty vivid activity so far beyond our concept of "life" as our concept of Godhead beyond ourselves.

Our life is ephemeral, as unworthy of notice as the dancing midge flies that live but for a day of sunlight. Our day is just as short in comparison with the awful span the individuals of the Elder race considered a life-span.

One of the terrible things to grasp about that time and that people is that EVEN THEY died, painfully gasped out their last breaths, the whole mighty social organism, in one blast of unexpected heat from the sun. I often wonder if that blast of heat did come so suddenly, or did it creep up gradually, and the caverns the result of their frantic efforts to escape the increasing terror of the sun. This could not be, because they had space ships - or did space ships come later? Was there then a smaller race followed them in space ships - but all that is speculation, and we are trying to stick to the facts we know. Their fight with the sun rays must have occupied many centuries, and the sun probably ended in one blast of mighty anger all their efforts.

I wish I could tell you how a man's footsteps echo and re-echo in the endless gleaming corridors of that titanic labyrinth that no man as we know him ever conceived or executed. I wish there were some way you could conceive of the immensity of those borings in which one can be lost forever to man's knowledge, in which one can travel for a lifetime of our days and never find a familiar thing or see the same scenes twice.

You have perhaps been lost in an office building? Then conceive of an office building multiplied by the area of the Earth, seamed across with monstrous chasms of earthquake faults; of tier on tier of river-wide highways which girdle the globe seven miles under the surface. Then space this vision one over the other several times, a score of times - and you begin to comprehend the immensity of the Elder building. There are levels on levels of these mighty borings, they are numbered and signed for traffic beyond little man's keeping track of his whereabouts in them. Under the sea are vast escape ports for submersibles, now covered over with an age of sediment. In our mountains are thousands of strange indentations which were once the entrances (the "Intramen" of the Elders) all weathered and burned away until we call them valleys or dells or canyons or what have you. But a good student of aerial maps could trace out many of their shapes - if he were credulous enough to look.

He must be that credulous. Man must inherit what is waiting there for him. The widest area's of earth have yet to be discovered: they are the levels of the Elder borings! (That is, officially discovered.) His own earth's greatest living room and finest treasures are a secret kept from him by some of the most frightfully ignorant and selfish of the four-limbed creatures called human.

The dog-in-the-manger who first conceived of keeping all the underworld a secret from surface men is their major prophet, is to their most widely spread religion what Christ is to Christianity!

Keeping that ancient evil compact has become the major instinct of the modern cavern man. They have stood against all progress for all surface men in the name of that prophet!

The dog-in-the-manger religion has down there one great rival. It is that religion known to us as Satanic. These, too, have their reasons for secrecy, their guilt to hide from avengers, and it is their one point of agreement - a point today dissolving before the light of a new common sense spreading among them all. Hence this book, and others that will follow.

THE HIDDEN WORLD

Now among us there are many who can think enough to know that there was an Elder race of great accomplishments beyond our own. These sane must realize that a man does not write whole volumes for the mere purpose of hearing himself talk about a subject of a size no brain could invent for the mere entertainment of credulous asses amongst our surface people.

These exceptional minds among us must realize in these words the profound and exact truth - THE ELDER RACE DID EXIST AND HAS LEFT US A VAST HERITAGE WHICH WE MUST CLAIM!

They DID bore the earth full of caverns, and those caverns have been for an age the dwelling place of secretive peoples who have carefully kept their vast secret from surface races.

When the Elder race perished from a solar prominence of immense size and the terrible heat it brought - these caverns were left intact and full of the machinery of life of a race technically advanced beyond our wildest dreams.

After that time came the capture of the moon. Long after. After that time came the so-called "Golden Age". After that time came the repeated deluges which swept man-life almost entirely out of existence more than once. After that time came the "sinking of Lemuria" and many another unrecorded and terrific change of life condition upon earth.

BUT THE INDESTRUCTIBLE MACHINERY REMAINED INTACT AND VERY MUCH IN REPAIR, AND IS USED STILL TODAY IN MOST AREAS OF EARTH!

What it could do for us all in benevolent hands (if such can be conceived as existing) is what it must do for us, and that must come to pass! At present it is not all in such hands - a very large part remains in the hands of people very reluctant to consider surface civilization as anything but an enemy and a threat to their way of life!

But I digress. There are a great many facts we can learn about the "big race" and if these facts get mixed with latter things, blame it on the confusion of times and tongues and periods of occupation - it cannot be helped.

Any bit of information you can acquire about our gigantic

forefathers is worth the effort, in understanding a past that was worthy of understanding - and not any sterile reflection of the insane goings on we call living today.

We ourselves are but a faint reflection left on the face of a dying time by the mighty life of the past. I work thus because I see that unless men learn to look this fact in the face, learn what they are and why they are headed for still another "world war" - they will never again become more than an ephemeral wavering reflection of the vivid reality of the past. A mere two-dimensional repetition of a thing once so mighty that it was by comparison, three-dimensioned.

The time of the Gods of earth's youth, that time is beyond any man's words to depict unless you assist in every way by exerting your utmost powers of imagination and deduction to completely visualize - not what I say, but what I mean to say!

If you are gifted with an insight greater than the wooden mental tools now in general use, you may deduce from my perhaps pitiful-even-to-you attempts something of the greatness that was, and could be again if we mastered the "big race's" secrets of life processes.

Many are so gifted, for they have in them the heredity of a people vastly superior to ourselves, complete with instincts aged into strength by eons of growth under better life conditions than we today comprehend exist anywhere.

If you seek and find the way, and avoid the death that waits the newchum in those endless halls, you will someday learn what life really was when earth-life was strong as eternity, beautiful as a vast multiple of the tiny weakling concept we employ when we say "lovely".

You will KNOW then that today's man is but a puny reflection of the mighty men of the early days of earth.

Time and seeded disintegrance of radioactivity have destroyed the seed-bed of life that earth was then, and now our seed-bed produces not men but the things we moderns call men.

Then they were vast and grew to god-like wisdom and gigantic strength. Now, we are puny worms who crawl for a moment and die and never gestate or grow our space-wings or learn to think as men were once born to think. We must face this ugly fact and turn toward the path they trod to greatness.

The pitiful unbelieving reaction of so many to my revelations (not my own, but from the caves) of the existence of the great races of the past has been my own criterion of the depth of modern man's fall.

"It could not have been because it was so great" seemed their reaction. We cannot believe such things, they are too big, they make our modern wonders look like trash! We can only believe little things."

Nevertheless I must try to tell you of the vast and ancient face of life that was when its components, the little energy exchanges of the cells, were perfect, and life grew without hindrance from nature, in vast fecundity.

Those were the days of the Covenant on earth.

All the great minds of ancient and long continued growth supported the Covenant, which gave each life its chance to develop and screened out each failure, even as Darwin's evolutionary processes are said to do today. In those days species were the product of intelligent manipulation toward fitness. Today we must rely on survival alone. That it is not enough, as one can deduce from the results of our wars.

I have written so many beginnings to this book - and not one of them says the important thing I want to get across.

I want to say this book has been scrambled by ray interference until it is unrecognizable even to me. This scrambledness has one virtue - it helps to prove my main message to you: there is an enemy who would rather you did not read such books. It would be vastly better if you were required to read it or burn, for that enemy must be exposed. Please remember, when the incoherent and scrambled state of this Mss. calls itself to your cross-eyed attention, that in itself proves the existence of the thing which this book is chiefly created to bring to your attention: the unseen enemy of your way of life.

The following is another beginning.

THE HIDDEN WORLD

BY WAY OF SMASHING THE generally-worn blindfold over most men's eyes, the following book has been dedicated to naked women, squalling cats and thunder and lightning.

(That ought to smash something.)

Now that you have read the first paragraph, I will assume that either the nude woman, the cat or the crash of electricity has pierced the usual wall between you and perception of the unwelcome details of plain living.

I started out to call this book Evil. I meant to talk as eruditely as an ordinary moron may of the things of glory that were once in life - how they have gone away before the influx of growing evil.

I meant to picture the pitiful NOW that we call life. I meant to picture by contrast all the things life might be, might have become, if we had retained our long vanished understanding of Evil and what it has done to us in the far past and what it does to us today.

I meant to picture what life will inevitably become because of the growing evil. What life could be, what it should be and what it will be. They are three very different pictures indeed.

At the end I meant to place no moral for anyone but this: Evil is an idiot, and the ways of evil are a total loss for any living thing.

However I am writing this book about the Elder World instead, because the world in the Elder time was so very greatly what it should be and is not at all today.

So when you note the clash of gears in my mental machinery, you will remember my alibi. I have several other excuses for the (very evident to me) shortcomings of this book. There is also the mental tamper from the "non-existent" ray employees who have orders to frustrate me and everyone like me from any successful publicizing of the Elder world and what it contains. I have included more or less extensive samples of this tamper, to show that it exists and as a curiosity of thought not before publicly exhibited for what it is.

I have had to make a book up out of heterogeneous notes,

because of this conflict, this "non-existent" hampering of mental effort. Such efforts as I have been able to make toward pulling the book together into unity may not prove very successful - for which I will not bore you with excuses.

At the end, you know, I will die for my writings. By some obscure method that will look like anything but murder - I shall die.

For we do have an evil exploiter, parasite (there is no adequate descriptive in our tongue), who is hidden from us by a thousand and more years of suberfuge. One cannot write of evil without mention of this enemy of our life, this living evil that rides earth to its death.

It is true that the enemies of earth's greatest evil (when they succeed in striking the thing that dogs each man of us who know) are killed by various "accidents". Their car upon the road is crashed; the disease that walks earth, unseen by any doctor of today, strikes them down. Like Pierre Curie, they walk into a van-load of booze and are crushed. Various are their deaths, but there is but one agent - the custom of secrecy inherent in all the thinking of the underworld.

I shall be glad when that time comes, for then I shall be free at last of them all. No more to watch what they do to my race. No more to know myself unable to strike a real blow in their defense, unable to do anything but write obscurely of "evil". I shall be very glad to meet their particular reaper.

After me, it may be that men will hear no more of their hidden parasites, their word for anathema that we have not, their unseen predators who do make of them a mock and a joke in all the ports of space.

"Ports of space"? Yes, there are space travelers on earth now, this day - and they have been on many a planet where the people of the surface are not barred from participation in the knowledge left by the Elder race. Where the people are a part of their state, where men and women are allowed to share in all the fruits of the past efforts of mankind - and not, as we, allowed only to produce and to know nothing of the wonder of the elder devices for pleasure and

976

culture and mental relaxation.

Yes, there are inhabited worlds out there who know of us, pity us, and would like to help us. One day they will manage it. But the time is not yet.

But I forget, I am speaking to an audience who expect no such mention of things they do not know about. So consider the phrase "ports of space" and the following phrases as having been unsaid. We will cross them out again. We will call them tamper, inserted by the unseen wight at his ray mech, to keep the mind of the reader closed to what is to come.

Then we will consider the wight and his ray as an insertion also, put in to explain what "may" lie under our feet in the rocks of our planet. The unexplored and "nonexistent" Elder World of which this book has been written. Consider the tamper and the ray and the lazy malevolent wight at his telemach as things inserted as was the woman and the cat and the thunder - to wake you up and make you think.

Men will read such errant scribblings only at the point of a gun, some still existent portion of my good sense exclaims to me.

Well, there is such a gun, and I will show it to you. Then you will see that I speak the truth; that I alone of all the myriad of would-be merchants of words was able to give you more than mere "words of wisdom"; was able to give you directions toward that mighty goal men seek when they pray, or marry, or prospect in the desert, or go into politics; was able to point out to you the path to that goal.

You will see that I alone saw the cause of the evil sickness and the blight that is visited upon your every act and every thought. Visited upon you all by those who would not see you prosper. If you men of the surface do see that, I will be great and rewarded. Of course, as is always the case with your best servants, that comes long after death. After I have gone, and the manner of my going been unnoted for the murder that it will be.

Usually such as I do die unnoticed, and their works are all destroyed and spirited away from the memory of man.

The LORELEI

By RICHARD S. SHAVER

IN EVERY ANCIENT myth and tale of the far past there appear those female harbingers of doom, the Lorelei. Using their beauty and unearthly sexual allure, they cause men's death . . . and every student wonders why such a beautiful tale of supernatural female attractions should also be so deadly, so evil, so unnatural.

To understand the Lorelei and why they are deadly to mankind, you have to go back in time to their first appearance.

In Edith Hamilton's capable work on Mythology, she says: "The Titans, often called the Elder Gods, were for ages supreme. . ." She also quotes from an ancient verse -

   "Strange clouded fragments of an ancient glory,
   Lost Halls of Heaven. . ."

All of these writings are pitiful to one who knows the truth about the false assumptions and even falser deductions that appear on the pages between the actual fragments of truth from the past.

THE HIDDEN WORLD

Hence the word "Lorelei", which in fact means "The lie about the Lore".

The myths and Edith Hamilton both tell us the Titans were the Elder race, and that is correct. They lived long ages of glorious life on early earth, before the Deluge. They built tremendously, and they bored earth's undercrust full of highways, a complete network of wonderful roads in tubes that reach every part of earth. Today these tubes are crushed in certain areas where earthquake faults cross their lines, and these areas contain the only unspoiled treasures from that far past. All the rest have been pawed over, so smashed and destroyed by ignorant vandals, many, many times warring through the caves in later times.

The myths tell us that Cronus ruled over these Elder Titans, until he was overthrown by Zeus.

Here enters the first Lore-lie. Zeus did not come along till long after the Titans had parished in the cataclysms that destroyed all the surface works of the Titans and caused the survivors to leave earth - if there were any survivors. It is generally deduced that some of the orginal race must have survived to be our ancestors. But this is not necessarily so. Since the Titans themselves had conquered space, may even themselves have been originally colonists from space, it is possible that our own ancestors came to earth from space after the death or departure of the original Titan race. Cronus was only the symbol for time, not a ruler.

Of course, your orthodox scholar discounts all of this, calls it all "nature myths", and pretends that there never existed in the past anything but an overwise ape with a club. However, they have to discount a few carloads of evidence proving quite the contrary (which they find no obstacle). Orthodox scientists have a logical explanation for everything.

There were only twelve great Olympians, who were supposed by the Greeks to dwell in Olympus. This fact of their low numbers, has been typical of all the "Gods", they have been most exclusive throughout history. There is a reason for this, based on their usual philosophy of scarcity, or out and out selfishness. That reason is the reason that

979

THE HIDDEN WORLD

has pinned Prometheus to his mountain peak in every mythology - he wants to give the divine fire to common man. The Gods have always preferred to keep immortality to themselves, and this customary policy of complete secretiveness and utter exclusiveness has given rise to most of mankind's troubles ever since the first "Olympian" conceived it.

Actually, we can never know where or when the custom of secrecy and exclusiveness began, as we can see it in every mythos. When God kicked Adam out of Paradise, it was because Adam and Eve knew about evil as well as good. It has always been underworld policy not to have anyone know about evil, for a very good reason.

Only twelve of them were allowed to use certain rays out of all those who dwelt in the caverns under Greece. These twelve seemed to all be relatives, and even their own children, of whom they seem to have had as many as Solomon, were shut out from this exclusive circle.

This business of the rays and the mech of the caverns has always been the great secret of the Gods. Their immortality was no masquerade, but all the rest of their performance throughout mythological history, is mostly what mere mortals term contemptible. For instance, their voices always seemed to come from out of the air, as if they were invisible, and when the poor Greeks climbed Olympus, where they claimed to dwell, there was nothing to be found but the bare mountain top and some boulders which only by a stretch of the imagination could be termed the Throne of Zeus. Many Greeks held these God voices in open contempt - quote: "Marpessa loved Idas, but was pursued by Apollo. Idas dared to fight Apollo. Zeus parted them, told Marpessa to choose. She chose the mortal, fearing that the God would not be faithful." "He who with a mocking laugh . . . hunts his prey. . ." end quote. It was a stupid Greek who did not know that the voices from the "Gods" were as apt to lie as to tell truth.

To quote again (page 27, Mythology by E.H.):

"He (Zeus) is represented as falling in love with one woman after another and descending to all manner of tricks

980

THE HIDDEN WORLD

to hide his infidelity from his wife." end quote.

This is typical of the behavior of almost all the Gods of that time; few of them seem to have any human concept of honor or decency. Human life itself is to them the cheapest of commodities, and that a lie can cause a mortal's death seems to have been considered by the Gods only a clever coup.

After all, they are only mortals, ephemerae . . . seems to have been their attitude. Wars and battles and riots are caused by the voices of the Gods throughout the Greek myths, apparently just for amusement.

Remember, there were only a dozen of them, immortal, hiding in their Elder caverns, keeping their secret, not telling that all about them lies the lore of a great race that would have made all the mortals like Gods if only they had gotten a chance to study it. All this occurred when, you ask? Let's see . . . the seige of Troy, brought about by certain airy lies, occurred aproximately 1174 B.C.

Hera, Zeus wife, seems to have been chiefly responsible for the Trojan war. She was one of the three when Paris gave the Golden apple to Aphrodite. She never forgave him, and her schemes and implacable enmity brought about the downfall of the whole Trojan race. This is typical of the behavior of the Gods always; their very existence was based upon a lie and everlasting trickery.

The truth about the origination of their God-like characters is particularly revealing of the reasons for their habitual despicable behavior. If you will think back, you will recall it was the custom of those early peoples to offer up animals to their Gods. These were usually bullocks, lambs, and frequently maidens; as the Gods like the tender flesh of maidens. These offerings were roasted on an altar, situated above, of all things, a sort of cave (if you will look up the construction plans for some ancient temples you will find under the altar a large concealed chamber, reached by a tunnel). When the devout had turned away their faces so as not to be blinded by the Gods' appearance, the meat disappeared into this opening behind the altar, where you can imagine what they did with it. Even their meals were

THE HIDDEN WORLD

a lie.

The Gods, of course, were often officiating priests at the temples. Just how they journeyed back and forth is a secret lost today, as it was concealed then to all but their victims. Perhaps the priests were always just servants of the Gods, but one wonders just how they got their supplies if they didn't themselves cart it from the temples. They were "glorious", those Gods of mythology, when you know the truth about their traffic.

Let us picture what must have been the actual life of these "mythical" Gods. Most of you have been raised with the idea that nothing of the kind ever really existed. Most of you really believe there is only one true "God", and that Christ is his son, etc. Most of you have been brought up with the idea that the myths are merely primitive fairy tales. However, such is not the actual case at all.

The Gods existed, they were the "front" the cavern people erected between themselves and discovery by those vigorous early surface races. Even with all the great ray weapons of the caverns to protect them, they seem to have feared surface men even then.

The cavern peoples were themselves the subjects of the "Gods", the Gods were the reigning families of the underworld kingdoms. Most of the cavern peoples were also mortals, being denied the use of those certain super-secret rays which render the user virtually immortal. It is therein lies the rub; it is this particular point upon which has hinged all history, particularly its most evil and destructive chapters. The thorn in the rose of immortality has always been . . . their bodies lived on and on . . . but let me quote one of the myths, which may explain the character of the Gods better than modern words. I quote (from Hamilton's Mythology):

"Tithonus, the husband of Aurora, . . . had a strange fate. Aurora asked Zeus to make him immortal. Zeus agreed. But she had not thought to ask also that he should remain young. So it came to pass that he grew old, but could not die.

At last in pity, the Goddess laid him in a room and left

982

THE HIDDEN WORLD

him, shutting the door. There he babbled endlessly, words with no meaning. His mind had gone with the strength of his body, he was only the dry husk of a man."

To Memnon, his son, a great statue was erected at Thebes, etc."

Thus it has always been with the gifts of the Gods, laden with a poison. That poison, evil intent. At the heart of that intent, a sort of supernatural selfishness . . . no one, but no one, can have the gift of immortality but only themselves. Oh, the Gods have been very exclusive.

All through the myths, you find the Gods fighting and dying among themselves for this secret. In the Norse, this particular angle of the life of the Gods is seen in the theft of the Apples of Idun by Loki. All the Gods began to wither away, the very next day after they missed their apples. They take out after Loki . . . but then, you must know the story.

Here is one of the strange coincidences of mythology, which may or may not have some great meaning. Always, apples are connected with the secret of immortality. In the Garden of Eden, it is an apple which brings about the expulsion. In Asgard, the apples of Idun hold the secret. And in Greece, we find the golden apple in the hand of Paris, who was probably a greater fool than he knew when he gave it to Aphrodite. It is possible that the Apple is a spherical container of some mighty potent material. It is even probable. The fall of Troy can be traced back to that apple.

A golden apple; hmmm. Something to think about, those apples, when you know about the caverns and the strange mechanisms they contain, as well as the Elder custom of giving everything they built the semblance of some living thing. The caverns are filled with the subterraneans' nostalgia for living things of the surface - a parcel wrapping machine is built in the likeness of two beautiful slaves of golden metal. The palaces of their rulers are usually upheld here and there by pillars whose appearance is nothing but that of a graceful tree trunk. There are gardens of metal shrubs laden with fruit that is nothing but ordinary gems. Poor Aladdin, he probably found the golden apples too bulky for his cummerbund.

Quote: "into this busy scene stole Medea, curious... As her eyes fell upon Jason, Cupid swiftly drew his bow and shot a shaft deep into her heart. It burned there like a flame and her soul melted with sweet pain... She stole back to her chamber, amazed and abashed." from "Mythology, Edith Hamilton."

Now what this sort of scene from the myths means to the ordinary reader is little enough - a pretty fairy tale that has no connection with actual occurrence on earth, probably.

Actually, this scene contains some of the most startling and important facts about the use and purpose of the ancient mech of the caverns. Medea was the princess of and heir to a great kingdom. Jason was also the heir to a king, a powerful and important man. Both of them were relatives and descendants of Gods, we are told.

Cupid's bow is the important thing - today the same device and its result is called a "hook", but it is used for the same purpose, to arouse that permanent sort of affection we call love. The modern man has no idea that true love can be aroused by a simple magnetic ray, but it can.

Cupid's bow is a very special device, used for no other purpose than hooking certain important people. Even in the ancient world that saw its use and development, it was a secret device, known to few, for to them Mother Nature was a sacred entity, only to be tampered with by the most inspired and most deeply intuitive hands. The heart of the device is a tuning coil built like a spring. When the spring is released, after being magnetically activated by the most potent of all their many types of generators of synthetic neural electric, the tuning coil vibrates through a whole gamut of neural energies, stimulating every single cell of the mind of the subjects. This stimulation is not in one particular frequency, as with ordinary stimulative frequencies used for ordinary pleasure, but due to the vibrant spring-like action of the tuning coil, runs through every possible variant of these spectrums of neural magnetics, from which fact arises the fact of Cupid's device being called a bow. This spring

THE HIDDEN WORLD

action gives off a sharp "twang" and "thrum" when released, sounding to the Greeks exactly like the release of an arrow from a hard drawn bow.

The "hook" called love, Mother Nature's own device by which the male is drawn to the female, is aroused by artificial stimulation when the beam from Cupid's bow touches the nerves of the body. The beam carries into the nerves and the mind this polarizing current, and this current is precisely those numerous nerve cell electrics which the body generates in the act of love.

Every gland and every cell of the mind and what we call the "heart" of the body, responds to this flow of suddenly aroused attractive magnetic. Moreover, to make the sudden attraction completely potent, and to assure that the "love" that results is not misdirected to some other recipient, the mechanism is set up beforehand by atunement to the recipient, in this case Medea. This atunement is a delicate adjustment, done with a bit of tape carrying the personal magnetic pattern of the body electric of Medea. The cells of the "victim, in this case Jason, are suddenly and completely polarized by this superimposed magnetic attraction, his whole body magnetic suddenly begins to vibrate to the body pattern, the magical fact of Love, the same sort of miracle that Nature works herself in her seeking after ever new and greater patterns of life is worked by the artful designer of this mechanism.

Jason is suddenly and completely snared, just as is Medea. As the Myth goes, they didn't bother giving Jason a dose of Cupid's dart, just Medea. In the Myth Hera and Cupid's mother weren't particularly interested in Medea or her future, they just wanted her to help Jason. So they didn't bother dosing Jason, and eventually he left her. But for love of him, Medea turned against her father and killed her own brother.

Mortals have, since time immemorial, been snared into various unwelcome marriages by the use of this device. Cupid's darts have been used always by the Gods to further their plans. The only trouble is, these plans of theirs seem always to have been of fleeting and unimportant character, a temporary interest in the affairs of surface men, to further some fancied idea of revenge, to discourage some seeker after the secrets of Forbidden Fruit, or to cause some war which they deem necessary to the entertainment of their superior, Jove or Zeus or Pluto, the great old God who must always be entertained. In this case it seems they hope to start an entertaining fracas between Medea's father and the crew of the Argosy, and they succeeded.

Medea could only end their pursuit of Jason's ship by slaughtering her brother and casting his body overboard. Thus did the Gods' malevolent interference in the affairs of men usually end, in some tragically dramatic incident of such completely despicable nature. So, it seems, does their interference in our affairs and today in tragedy, in war, in the mismating of opposites in marriage - and all to the end that some malevolent old fixture of the "immortal" bandwagon should be entertained with our desperation.

However, the device itself, called Cupid's bow, was developed by the Elder race for one purpose only, to insure "proper" marriage. That is, in their political set-up, by the use of Cupid's bow, they insured that the leaders of opposed factions should fall in love and marry, and they insured that genetic factors were observed in the matings of their young couples. Thus by its use they developed ever better natures in their people, better brains and handsomer bodies. And they used it to bring about peace, for it is hard to quarrel with someone you love deeply.

Now I quote again, to show how it is used, even today. Remember that this particular scene took place some twelve to thirteen centuries before Christ. Well over three thousand years ago, and the existence of these devices and the "Gods" who use them in their hidden caverns is still secret to the surface peoples of earth. Those mechanisms were built of imperishable metal, to endure the ignorant usage and everlasting abuse of time itself, for they are still functioning today. But today the Gods are really warring with each other over the last remnants of the mighty work of the Elder race, and the study of their science and their machine art is still put off while the last of the "Gods" wallow in the stim and the ben-rays and call themselves immortal and look down upon surface man as ephemerae of no importance. Yet they themselves cannot and will not try to understand that they have to study and work to preserve the science that built those mechanisms or forever lose their use.

Quote: "As soon as he heard the message, Jason started. As he went Hera shed radiant grace upon him, so that all who saw him marveled at him. When he reached Medea it seemed to her as if her heart left her to go to him..."

Now note carefully the difference between seeming fact of occurrence and what was actually taking place, and does take place today.

What was actually taking place was a heterodyning of Jason's normal body aura, over a beam between Hera's mech and his own body, the mechanism augmenting this aura into a magentic field of great power around him. This is no more mysterious or difficult a miracle than is observed by all of you when you tune your radio in to the local station. It is just that the "miracle" is taking place using frequencies which have been made taboo to the surface race of mankind. The mechanism adds certain frequencies to the normal body aura which give an indicative power, i.e. - it states the fact of grace to the mind of the observer in abstract thought, just as plain and far more convincingly than any words could say it - "this man is utterly graceful" - thus - "Hera shed radiant grace" upon Jason literally. The myths are not, when so seen by those who know of the fact of the secret mechanisms, nearly so enigmatically miraculous or so utterly false, are they? Hera's radiant grace was shed by simple radio-augmentation, just as your radio takes a weak signal out of the air and augments it into a deafening music from the station.

Thus was Jason made overpoweringly attractive to Medea. Her "heart", i.e. the nerves of her young body, were already polarized to this attraction, her defenses were already destroyed by Cupid's bow and arrow, and when Jason walks toward her, the fact of love springs to life and her whole being flames - and will so flame for Jason to the end of her days. Yet, gentle reader, left to Nature, neither Medea nor Jason would have had the slightest interest in each other. Jason was an ignorant warrior who loved nothing so much as himself and his prowess in hunting and war, while Medea was a student of dark and difficult arts, and must have had access to the writings of the Elder race to be versed in "magic" as a knowledge of science was called in those days.

As we read on through this tale of the Argonauts, and see how the Gods treated Medea and Jason after they reached Greece, the full picture of the Gods' attitude toward mankind is brought out. Jason, after fathering two children by Medea, gallivants off to Corinth, apparently dragging Medea and her children along. We have to remember that Jason is the Golden Boy of Greece, the great hero, the man who has returned from what was equivalent to a voyage around the known world . . . and the very first such voyage made after the great Deluge. The Deluge had changed the geography of earth, and the new tribes of men springing up everywhere knew nothing of its geography.

But there were among them people like Medea who had studied the books left by the men who lived before the Deluge, and who knew the old geography and something of the science of the past. These people, as was Medea, were called sorcerers and magicians, witches and warlocks, by the ignorant of earth, and were often casually destroyed - in fact almost invariably were destroyed, for the "Gods", then as now, did not want surface mankind to know anything.

Thus we see that Cupid's darts sent into Medea, to cause her to love the ignorant and mean-natured Jason, eventually wrought her destruction, and we suspect that the whole thing came about because the Gods wanted Medea destroyed.

Thus Jason, a great-bodied "hero" of that time, proves in the end to have no real character at all, turns against Medea and decides to marry the daughter of the king of Corinth.

Corinth, if you know your Greek history, was the very richest city of Greece, in that time far surpassing Athens or any other city of earth in power and magnificence. To marry the Princess of Corinth was equivalent in our time to marrying a DuPont, if that DuPont happened to be a woman who owned most of New York City.

So we have the picture of poor dark-tressed Medea, home nursing two small children, being abandoned by a husband who loves to loll at court being idolized by the sycophants of the King of Corinth. When Jason gets around to telling her he means to marry the king's daughter, Medea loses her temper. Who can blame her?

She prepares a shirt of Nessus and sends it to the girl. And here we come to another phenomena of that far time, the shirt of Nessus. Nothing in our experience can act that way but radioactives! Did such as Medea have a knowledge of radioactives? There is no way to know today, since every library in history has been burned, not once but over and over. We really have almost no knowledge of that time but these few myths, which we disregard entirely.

Then Medea kills her two children by a faithless husband and takes off through the air in a fiery chariot. We suspect these fiery chariots drawn by dragons as later embellishments of fancy, but when so many wonders we had always considered pure flights of fancy prove upon closer examination to have been not fancy but fact, there must have been an occasional use of some sort of flying machine in that early time. It is quite possible that there were a few devices left about by the departing Elder race which could fly through the air, and that the common man should call them fiery dragons is no different from what the first airplanes were called by primitives in such places as Borneo.

But what I especially wanted to bring out was the God's treatment of their pawns, no different today than it was then. Poor Medea, trapped into unnatural love by Cupid, betrays her father, kills her brother, and in the end has to kill her own two children, just to entertain the Gods watching her on their telescreens in their hidden caves.

There you have the true reason and the means of understanding the "Gods" activity, in that phrase - "on their telescreens". To them, sitting in opulent idleness forever, the telescreen was like our TV. The only way they can change channels and get another program is by manipulating the poor people of the surface. So there sprang up among them a profession, a calling - the manipulators of mankind were their dramatists, who plotted out the tragedies and comedies of life for the entertainment of their masters, and then proceeded to bring it all about by manipulation.

Thus the tale of Jason and Medea was just a play, to them. They made of it what they call a "cacklepack". A "cacklepack" is an arrangement of thought records, which when placed in what they call a "dream mech", produces in three dimensions and in complete accompaniment of thought, smell, word, music, sound and the whole gamut of emotion, more real than reality, precisely what was recorded. This is an art among them; the production of these records is almost their only lucrative business, and the "cacklepackers" peddle their wares everywhere among the rich loafers in the caverns.

To them it means nothing that perhaps the greatest scientific mind of her time, Medea the sorceress, was put through a veritable Hell of tangled emotional responses; it is "just a play", the usual sort of thing all surface people are good for. It made no difference who died or how many, or how horribly or meanly they died; it was just a performance to them, making their cacklepacks. Thus today, we can trace the fine hand of the cacklepackers as they manipulate present day events, causing wars and turmoils, the more dramatic and tragic and bloody the brawl becomes, the better they like it.

Today, even, we produce the great Greek play about Medea without the slightest understanding of what it really means to us. Yet we pride ourselves we have risen above that dark time of ignorance. We think we have progressed, that modern times are less tragic, and we ignore the Gods as always.

Why, Medea probably knew more than our finest scientists, for she knew of the existence of the Lore of the Great Race of prediluvean times and had had opportunity to study some of their work, as proven by her knowledge of drugs and magic. You must note too that her brother was killed, and we can only surmise that her own fate was probably death. That she flew off through the air and escaped Jason's vengeance is hard to credit; in reality he probably killed her and concealed the deed with a lie.

Today we think we know so much, yet in many ways we are more ignorant than those same people of Colchis and of Corinth. They knew their Gods and they resisted their foul work upon the pattern of their lives, for the myths tell us time and again of certain ones who fought against the Gods and who were destroyed.

Think what Colchis would have become if the wise Medea had become its ruler! Think what Jason would have become if he had remained faithful to her and had learned some of her wisdom! The Gods have always destroyed the seeds of the future, planted in such people as Medea by Mother Nature herself, who creates her geniuses only to have the Gods destroy them . . . and the great Gods destroy them out of fear and utter baseness of character, not out of a desire to create a character play, or a tragedy. Among themselves they pretend they only do these deeds for entertainment, perhaps. But one knows better, in one's heart. The Gods and the Devils fear mankind, with a despicable baseless fear. They fear us because we are young and alive, while they are ancient husks from the past, clinging like leeches to life and fearing everything young with a desperation born of disease.

They fear us because inexorably age creeps up in their ancient bodies, they fear us because the aging mechanisms themselves generate a strange vibrant the Elder race called De, and this De, which is disintegrant energy, harbors in their bodies and will not be evicted. De is the enemy of immortality, De spoils all their pleasures with its deadening damper, De soils all their emotions, De moves in their minds with a malevolent will of its own and De causes their malevolent actions in truth.

The Gods have beneficial vibrants which keep them alive in spite of De, but all the beneficial in the world, (and today the old mechanisms are not so potent as once they were) cannot save them from this personal devil they inherit from their way of life. The Devil is a Devil because

De has replaced his natural good will with a will of its own. And the Gods are despicable because they too have not been immune from an accumulation of this De upon the films of their mind. Detrimental energy is a false will when it replaces original will in the lipoid films of the mind. But when they allow it to rule their every action, the difference between a God and a Devil is Nil. Thus I say, the Gods and the Devils are one today, and we can trust nor depend on neither one.

Beyond the Verge

HOME OF THE TEN LOST TRIBES OF ISRAEL

By DE WITT C. CHIPMAN

CHAPTER I.

ORATONGA.

THE OLD traditions, with their mingled truth, fable, and myth, extend back into Cimmerian darkness. The origin of the Mound Builders, and Chickimecs, has no written history.

According to their traditions, the first sunlight of time, shining on the races of man, streamed on the brown-faced Mound Builders and the black-eyed Chickimecs.

If we credit their story, in these remote ages, the rivers were then creeks, the lakes ponds, and the mountains were hills. Each claimed to have been always on the earth, coeval with each other, and to have been enemies from time immemorial. Whether the Mound Builders sprung from Egyptian, Japan, Malaysian stock, or were indigenous to the American continent, has never been settled. The same may be said concerning the Chickimecs, though the prevailing opinion is, that they were probably the oldest on the American continent.

THE HIDDEN WORLD

It is only necessary to refer to them so far as they relate to the lost Tribes of Israel, and this is limited to their doings with Oratonga, Emperor of the Chickimecs, as related in this chapter. The Mound Builders were sun-worshipers and sacrificed human beings. At the height of their power they had one religion, but in time they degenerated into worshipers of the serpent, buffaloes, bears, elks, eagles, mastodons, and Koneta, or the Evil One.

This apostacy from the ancient faith is readily seen in their mounds, and these crumbling earthworks are all that is left to commemorate this vanished race.

While united, they had driven the Chickimecs out of all North America south of Lakes Superior, Huron, Erie, Ontario, and the St. Lawrence river. A long peace or truce followed, but during that period the Chickimecs, after years of preparation, fell upon the Mound Builders simultaneously with three grand armies. Oratonga, their emperor, inflamed their minds by an appeal to love of native land, and an appeal to their sensual appetites. He pictured in glowing colors the beautiful country along the rivers of the south land, where flow the Scota, Miami, White River, Wabash, and Mississippi. He told of the lovely valleys, winding streams of the "sunny South," the luscious tropical fruits along the Southern Gulf, and promised them concubines among the dark-eyed and beautiful Mound Builders. Oratonga led the eastern army, Modaruska the middle, and Assiniboin the western. The countries now known as Ohio, Indiana, Illinois, Michigan, Wisconsin, Iowa, and Minnesota, were in the hands of the Chickimecs. Towns, fields, villages, and nagumbas, were given to pillage and flame. Such fearful slaughters were committed, that down into Indian language comes a tradition of "the dark and bloody ground."

There is scarcely a sacrificial, residential, monumental, historic, military, or inexplicable earthwork, but has some sad and pathetic memento of this dreadful tumult.

During seven years of blood and flame in which this terrible war had progressed, and up to the time our narrative commences, the most merciless and exterminating contest burst with the besom of destruction upon the Mound

994

Builders. Their prestige and spirit had been broken, their defeated and dispirited armies had been driven south of the Ohio, and west of the Mississippi, and the three conquering armies of invasion met, and were consulting about a crusade beyond these rivers, and while thus assembled, the first event in the history of this book is about to open, and all that follows relates solely to the lost Tribes of Israel.

Oratonga, surrounded by his officers and priests, gazed with rapt attention upon a strange and marvelous appearance in the east.

From the high ground on which they stood there was an extended view. On the top of the highest roll of the prairie his tent was pitched. For miles, to the right and left, his proud army was encamped. In front was a gentle descent down to a sluggish stream, fringed with grass and water plants. Beyond the stream the ground gradually ascended and stretched away into a broad prairie country, and over all this far-extended space a peculiar cloud was lowering, so dark as to exclude the direct rays of the sun. The cloud was half a mile high; it did not quite touch the ground. Above it was a clear sky, and far above that a few cumulous clouds floated here and there, and between them the fathomless blue reached up towards heaven.

But all around this peculiar dark cloud, above it, and underneath it, for a few feet above the ground, light was visible, but the body itself was so dense that nothing could be seen in it or through it. At the right and left the black clouds reached the ground, hanging like a dense curtain, thus cutting off the sight from the flanks and rear, and only at the front could anything be seen. What was inexplicable, thousands of men were marching in regular order with banners up, and from the midst of the cloud, but unseen, came the sound of horns, trumpets, and drums. They were not warlike sounds, but such as are heard when people are at peace and marching on some civic, social, or semi-military occasion.

A line of pale, wavering, mysterious phosphoric light played through the darkness, giving it a most peculiar and impressive appearance; and now and then this light disclosed for an instant the banners and shining spears far back in the cloud of marching men as they swayed from side to side, and rose and fell with the inequalities of the ground.

While Oratonga was absorbed in witnessing this remarkable spectacle, the cloud shot down to the ground and darkness hid all from sight, and only the sound of martial music could be heard rolling out of the darkness.

The face of Oratonga betrayed surprise and perplexity, but not fear. In a few words he commanded his army to be "formed in battle array," and in an incredibly short period of time there was formed, to the right and left, and down the slope, and on the edge of the plain, a mighty line of battle many miles long. Suddenly the cloud, lifted over the advancing host, gradually disappeared, and the sunshine disclosed a mighty army arranged around a tent-like structure, over which hovered a spiral cloud, rising straight up to the sky and reaching beyond human sight. What did all this wonderful spectacle mean? Clearly these were not Mound Builders, their hereditary enemies. The terrible defeat they had recently met at his hands would have demoralized them completely from some time to come. Besides, hundreds of women, children, and domestic animals were among them. It was clearly not his hereditary enemies. Turning to a high officer near him he said:

"What does all that mean? How could such a host appear without our knowledge? What are scouts worth?"

To which the officer replied:

"They came through the lands of the Mound Builders. Our scouts tell of a strange people, protected by fire and clouds, traveling northward, and the Mound Builders, by the advice of their highest priests, have given them safe conduct, as they seem to be protected from the skies, and, if need be, they become invisible to scouts, hid by such a dark cloud as we just beheld. They harm none if let alone, but no one can stand before them. You see yonder cloud piercing the heaven; when it moves forward they all march, and when the cloud stops they halt and remain until it moves again, and thus they alternately march and encamp."

"How did you get this information?"

"It is from our spies and scouts, but no one gave it credit or consideration sufficient to report, no one believed it, nor did I until this day, and this moment, but my eyes converted me."

"I will go," said Oratonga, "to the bottom of this, but ha! what is that?"

A loud blare of a trumpet was heard, the advancing cloud halted, the host encamped, a movement was seen in the extreme front, and a solitary person passed through the nearest line of soldiers, with a white flag in his hand, and was now slowly approaching them.

He was of a sedate and venerable appearance, dressed in priestly robes, such as had never been seen by Oratonga or his people before. He came leisurely along, without any appearance of hesitation or fear, as if he was lord of the land.

On his head was a high priestly cap, and on his breast shone precious stones of twelve different kinds, which blazed and flashed with a brilliancy almost dazzling. His garments were of fine linen, significant of earth. The blue denoted the sky, being like lightning in its pomegranate, and in the noise of his bells, resembling distant thunder. And as for the Ephod, it showed God had made the universe of four elements, and the interwoven gold related to the splendor by which all things are enlightened. The breastplate, in the middle of the Ephod, was to represent the earth. The girdle signified the ocean, which goes around the earth.

The turban surmounting his head was blue, and signified heaven, and the name of God was inscribed upon it. With breastplate, Ephod, turban, and girdle, and dressed in fine linen, with chains of gold and rings, this person presented a brilliant and imposing appearance.

But over and above all other things were four rows of engraved stones, three in a row, twelve in all, as shown at his feet in the drawing. Each stone was set in a rim of gold, like a cameo, or head pin, with a button or stud, through which chains of gold wire held the Ephod in position, and these stones were called the URIM and THUMMIM, from which priests in the Ark and before the Altar discerned the will of God.

As this strange person approached, the outer sentinels and scouts of Oratonga's army gave way, and he approached unchallenged. Seeing this, Ten Osta, one of the leaders of the Altonga giants said:

"So, my lord, they all give way before yonder person. He goes unchallenged. Had my brave Altongas been across his path it would not have been so."

"This is evident. Discipline and vigilance must be preserved. Ten Osta, take a band of Altongas, halt that person, and demand who he is, what of his people, and his purpose, and, Ten Osta, see that he halts, and that he waits our pleasure."

Delighted at the command, the giant lifted to his lips the hollow thigh-bone of a slain Mound Builder, which hung at his side, and blew ten, harsh, quick notes, which demanded a hundred men, and hurried towards his command. A sudden commotion was seen among the giants, and a hundred fierce warriors, with their heavy war hammers and spears, met Ten Osta on a run.

He halted them, and with a sharp command to the right, and, at their head, with long strides and resolute faces they all swept towards the solitary man.

The balance of the Altongas, the grand army in battle array, Oratonga and his officers, looked with absorbing interest towards the solitary traveler and the giants, fast approaching each other. The stranger had crossed the sluggish stream, and was one third of the way to the foot of the rise, along and across which stood the army of Oratonga.

In the distance was the strange host; above them rose the cloud, reaching out of sight, into the heavens. On this side magnificent army of Oratonga, with rank behind rank, and row after row, with glittering spears, and battle-axes, all gazing upon Ten Osta and the solitary but unconcerned traveler.

Ten Osta, when within speaking distance, cried out in a loud voice:

"Halt, stranger! Your name! Your people! Your purpose, I demand!"

unaltered pace towards the headquarters of Oratonga. The army was astonished, and some of them petrified with fear, except the Altongas. When they saw the fire go out as suddenly as it appeared, and Ten Osta disappear, they believed it was some magic or illusion of the mind, or some diabolism which could be counteracted by numbers, or dauntless courage at the battle of the palisades with Koolkan, commander of the Mound Builders will not be surprised at their action on this occasion. And being in battle array, they determined to revenge or rescue their beloved commander, and so the three front ranks, with leveled spears, rushed headlong, shouting their terrible battle-cry, upon the mysterious stranger. He stopped, looked upon the wild charge, faced them and said:

"Oh, foolish mortals, will you never fear the Lord?"

When the shouting Altongas had passed through the lines, and were sweeping towards him, the stranger looked up, made a downward movement of both hands, and said:

"JEHOVAH!"

Suddenly the ground opened, and with cries of fear and despair the three lines plunged headlong into the awful chasm, deeper than any man could see. The ground closed, and only a line of disrupted soil, where no grass was seen, remained as evidence of the tragic fate of the fierce and foolish Altongas.

The other three lines, who did not charge, fell back from the line of battle, aghast, while a benumbing fear seized upon all who had witnessed these two marvelous manifestations of omnipotent power.

As the stranger pursued his steady course, when he reached the line of soldiers, they gave way right and left, making a long lane, from the foot of the rolling ground up to the highest part, where the astonished Oratonga and his officers stood. Among all the thousands in the grand army of Oratonga, who witnessed these wonders, there was but one who was not intimidated and speechless with fear. A young priest named Nardo. From youth he had been pious, fearless, and could speak all languages he had yet encountered. When he beheld these wonderful displays they tallied so completely

Without halting, the stranger said, as he still advanced,

"Fall back, open the way, we want a peaceable passage to the Northland, where we go by the direction of our Prophets and JEHOVAH."

"Halt, I say," cried Ten Osta, "or you will be transfixed by these spears."

Mortal, who can stand before the great Jehovah's agent? Once more I say stand back! Open the ranks, and let me through."

"Audacious stranger, again, and the last time, I say halt!" And Ten Osta advanced with his enormous war hammer uplifted, and his savage face lit with anger and surprise, while the distance between them was not more than twenty feet.

The stranger, with his right hand uplifted, and still advancing without pausing, made a sudden and impulsive movement forward. Ten Osta was hurled backwards, falling headlong to the ground, his battle-ax was whirled far away, and without halting the stranger advanced, throwing both hands upwards and out, right and left. The spears of the one hundred men were hurled upwards, cast right and left; the warriors whirled round and round like a whirlwind passing through a mass of chaff. For a brief time they lay stunned and helpless, then sprung to their feet, chagrined and angry, and at the command of Ten Osta, who had risen with a shout of savage ire, they rushed towards the stranger, who still continued his steady course towards the astonished lines of Oratonga. Hearing the fierce cries of Ten Osta and his men, he turned, and beholding their savage looks and long leveled spears he lifted both hands and said,

"JEHOVAH!"

Suddenly, like a flash of light coming from where, no one could tell, a fierce, devouring, and all-consuming flame flared over Ten Osta and his men, and when the stranger lowered his hands the fire disappeared, and Ten Osta and his hundred men were gone, and were never seen again. The ground where they stood was black as a cinder, and no remains of soldiers, battle-axes, or spears could be seen. Turning calmly, the stranger recommenced his steady and

1000

with his ideas of a Supreme Being, that he exclaimed with rapture, "Wonderful, sublime!" And hastening forward, he met the stranger with open arms, who gravely saluted him, placed his hand upon his head, and said:

"The peace of God be yours, and may His spirit fill your soul now and evermore! Selah!"

All who witnessed the meeting between the stranger and Nardo felt an instantaneous relief, and the mortal fear gradually left them, and soon the stranger stood in the presence of Oratonga. Whatever might have been the feelings of that redoubtable warrior, he was too diplomatic and shrewd to display them, and he said:

"You come, doubtless, the envoy and representative of the strange people yonder," and Oratonga pointed to where their encampment was seen. "And whether you come in peace or in war, you will find us, just in one, and fearless in the other. I await your pleasure!"

"O king, warrior, or emperor, as the case may be, I am but an humble prophet of the most high God, known in my land as King of Salem, which is king of peace. Without father, without mother, without descent, having neither beginning of days nor end of life; but made like unto the Son of God; abideth a priest continually." (Hebrews 7:1-4).

"In the Book of books I am called Melchisedec, and yonder is the Tabernacle, the Ark of Jehovah, with the Mercy-seat, the Pot of Manna, Aaron's Rod, and the Ten Commandments. We are of the seed of Abraham, and of God the Father, the Great 'I Am that I Am,' who has in the past shown Israel many blessings and curses. We have broken the covenant, but a few of us have been faithful, and He has directed us through our prophets, to follow yonder cloud, by day," and he pointed towards it, "and the pillar of fire by night, to the north end of the earth. We have been years on the way, and now all we ask of you is permission to travel, peacefully and unmolested, through your dominion. We will not trouble your people for provisions, for the Lord our God supplies all our wants, and his manna feeds us when other provisions fail. I have spoken, and I await your answer."

After a moment's hesitation, Oratonga said:

1001

"King of Salem! you say, that means peace. That is all the passport you need through the land of Oratonga. Though you see me at the head of a mighty army, it is to recover our native land, which the Mound Builders have held by force and conquest for centuries; but I prefer peace, and when you say that you are the 'King of Peace,' it shall be your passport from here to the Northland or to the North Sea."

As Oratonga ceased, Melchisedec said:

"'Tis well! One of our omnipotent prophets has said, 'He that liveth by the sword, shall die by the sword.' You are surrounded by a mighty army, spears, battle-axes, and swords are visible, as far as the eye can see; in warring for your own native land, do not encroach on your neighbor, for if you trespass over the boundaries that God has marked for all nations, you will be destroyed."

Oratonga waved his hand along the battle-line, and proudly said:

"These are mine, and a hundred times more if needed, to fight on our own, or on another's land."

"True, true," said Melchisedec; "but they all belong to Jehovah. You saw a hundred men and Ten Osta disappear in flames. You saw three lines of battle swallowed up, and the Great I Am could annihilate you and all your army as suddenly, if He so willed; who can limit the power of Him who made all things?"

After a moment's hesitation, Oratonga said:

"King of Salem, I am not diposed, after what I have seen, to doubt the power of the one you call 'I Am.' Tell me more of Him! The Emperor of the Chickimecs would learn more."

"Emperor of the Chickimecs," replied Melchisedec, "the great Jehovah, the I Am, made the world, the sun, moon, stars, He raised the lofty mountains above the clouds, marked with His finger the channel of the rivers, hollowed out the beds of the lakes, He holds the winds in His hands, the lightning obeys His nod, He notes the falling sparrow, enumerates the hairs of our head, He knows the secret thoughts of man's mind, He tries the reins of every heart, rewards or punishes man, according to his deeds. He called Abraham, promised his seed should be like the sands on

1002

the seashore, the stars in the sky, if they would keep His covenant. They did for a time, but proved recreant, were enslaved, repented, and He led them to the land of promise, performing many wonderful miracles, crossing the Red Sea and Jordan, dry-footed, while Pharaoh and his hosts were overwhelmed and drowned. Water spouted at the touch of Moses' rod, Kingdoms were overthrown, armies destroyed and swallowed up in the earth; and many wonderful and miraculous things done to manifest His power, and to protect us. But we failed to keep our part of the covenant, our nation has been overthrown and disrupted. We are to be scattered among all people, but a few of us, the faithful from all the ten tribes, have the Tabernacle and the Ark of the Covenant, and the sacred things locked up in it, and we are on a journey to the Northland, where we are to disappear until the fullness of time when our Messiah shall come, and Israel shall be collected at Jerusalem.

"After Titus took Jerusalem, all our people except us were to be scattered among the nations, but they will assimilate with none in faith and religion. They will be obedient to the government of their residence, but loyal evermore to the religion of Moses, Abraham and Jehovah; they will never be absorbed, never blend religiously, but in all ages, climes and countries, will be miraculously saved. Like Moses in the Nile, Daniel in the lions' den, Shadrach, Meshach and Abed-nego in the fiery furnace, they will remain undestroyed. And among nations will be an ever-present and living miracle of the truth of God's care for His chosen people. They were typified in the burning bush, maltreated, abused, banished, persecuted but undestroyed."

"King of Salem," said Oratonga, "you tell a wonderful story. It would surpass human credulity to believe. But when I remember Ten Osta, and my gallant Altongas, I am not prepared to controvert anything you may say; but why should your people be selected as the chosen, indestructible, immortal, and favored nation?"

"For two good reasons, O Emperor," replied Melchisedec. "First, ours was the most degraded, impure, filthy, stiff-necked and rebellious people, and to show His power,

1003

He took us from slavery and fitted us for heaven, and to be an example for all mankind. And, second, for the reason that men had forgotten that there was but one God, just, pure, omnipotent, merciful, and ready to forgive the repentant, and while all the world worshiped idols, and had a multitude of filthy and immoral gods and goddesses, the Jew was taken from slavery and sin, educated to teach the world that there was but one God, mighty, all powerful, pure, a hater of sin, who (after purifying the Jew) made him worthy of heaven, and taught him that a Messiah should come to Jew and Gentile alike; who should redeem the repentant from sin, and now a few of the faithful with myself are going to the North country; led by a cloud by day, and a pillar of fire by night; protected from all foes by the great Jehovah, and relying upon the promises found in our prophetical books, wherein He promises to bring us out from among the nations where we are scattered; and the promise is to bring us out of the North land, where we were to remain hidden until the Messiah comes, and Jerusalem is restored." The radiant face, and shining countenance of Melchisedec was lit with a light almost celestial.

"King of Salem," said Oratonga, "the more you tell me the more you interest me, and if it is your pleasure, I would be glad to hear something about your prophets, and the reasons which impel you to travel northward, where all is ice, frost, and eternal snow."

"Emperor of the Chickimecs, nothing gives a prophet of God more pleasure than to lift the veil and disclose to attentive rulers the decrees which the Lord God discloses to him."

At this Oratonga, and a few of his leading warriors and priests went into the Emperor's tent, where Oratonga seated himself upon his throne, had a seat drawn in front of him upon which Melchisedec was seated, and facing the emperor he said:

"O Emperor, among our people are certain men, renowned for austere, temperate, and moral lives, who walk daily in spiritual communion with God, who fills them with a divine and resistless impulse, which impels them to speak

1004

and write, and we call them Prophets. The greatest of these was Moses, who led our people from bondage, and he went up on a mountain and remained forty days and nights talking to God face to face, and he learned how God made the firmament, world, dry land and sea, sun, moon, and stars, and all things throughout the universe; then he came down from the mountain, bringing the Ten Commanments written on stone, and the face of Moses shone with a glorious light like that of the sun, and so light and dazzling that it would have blinded men, had he not covered it with a mantle. Moses gave us our law, our religion, to which we have ever since adhered, and will while time continues. He brought us to the promised land, was buried by angels in an unknown grave. Since then we have a line of prophets; and many of them have prophesied about our going to the Northland, the restoration of the Jews; and as we are now journeying towards this Northland, I will speak what our Prophets say concerning that, discarding all other matters.

" 'Behold, I will bring them from the North country, and gather them from the coasts of the earth . . . a great company shall return thither.' - Jeremiah, 31:8. 'Behold, I will gather them out of all countries, whither I have driven them in my anger, and in my fury, and in great wrath, and I will bring them again unto this place, and I will cause them to dwell safely.' - Jer. 32:37. 'For I will take you from among the heathen, and gather you out of all countries, and will bring you into your own lands. And ye shall dwell in the land that I gave your father; and ye shall be my people.' - Ezekiel, 34:13; Jeremiah, 23:3. 'And I will make one nation in the land upon the mountains of Israel; and one king to them all; and there shall be no more two nations, neither shall they be divided into two kingdoms any more at all.' - Ezek. 37:22. 'And thou shalt come from thy place out of the north parts, thou, and many people with thee, all of them riding upon horses, a great company, and a mighty army.' - Ezek. 38:15. 'And it shall come to pass that as ye were a curse among the heathen, O house of Judah, and house of Israel, so will I save you, and ye shall be a blessing; fear not, but let your hands be strong. . . And men shall dwell in it, and there

1005

shall be no more utter destruction; but Jerusalem shall be safely inhabited.' - Zech. 8:13; 14:11. 'I have raised up one from the North, and he shall come: from the rising of the sun, shall he call upon my name: and he shall come upon princes as upon mortar, and as the potter treadeth clay.' - Isaiah, 41:25. 'The remnant of Israel shall not do iniquity, nor speak lies; neither shall deceitful tongues be found in their mouth, for they shall feed and lie down, and none shall make them afraid.' 'And I will gather the remnant of my flock out of all countries whither I have driven them, and will bring them again to their folds; and they shall be fruitful and increase.' 'But the Lord liveth which brought and which led the seed of the house out of the North country, and from all countries whither I had driven them; and they shall dwell in their own country.' 'And it shall come to pass afterward, that I will pour out my spirit upon all flesh; and your sons and your daughters shall prophesy, your old men shall dream dreams, your young men shall see visions. . . . And I will show wonders in the heavens, and in the earth, blood, and fire and pillars of smoke. - Joel 2:28,30.' While we follow the cloud and pillar, it shall lead us to a land described by Isaiah, 60:18 to 22: 'Violence shall no more be heard in thy land, wasting nor destruction within thy borders; but thou shall call thy walls salvation, and thy gates praise. The sun shall no more be thy light by day; neither for brightness shall the moon give light unto thee: but the Lord shall be unto thee an everlasting light, and thy god thy glory. Thy sun shall no more go down: neither shall the moon withdraw itself: for the Lord shall be thine everlasting light, and the days of thy mourning shall be ended.' 'For as the new heaven and the new earth, which I will make, shall remain before me, saith the Lord, so shall your seed and your name remain.' Isaiah 66:22. 'And it shall come to pass that from one new moon to another, and from one Sabbath to another, shall all flesh come to worship before me, saith the Lord.' - Isaiah 66:23.

"You see, O Emperor, that the land where we are traveling is northward, where violence shall cease, where there shall be neither sun nor moon, nor stars, but there shall be everlasting light."

1006

"Prophet of him whom you call Lord, Jehovah and God," said Oratonga, "you have filled me with wonder; but according to our prophets you state things which I neither comprehend, nor the wisest philosophy of the Chickimecs can understand."

"Mortal man," said Melchisedec, "do you not know that philosophical minds are seldom sound in belief, they generally are sceptics in religion. Because the dissecting-knife cannot find the soul, the so-called scientific physician denies its existence. Who can comprehend sight, speech, hearing, intelligence, goodness, or evil? - no knife in the hand of the surgeon can find these, and no philosopher will deny their existence; but your so-called philosophers become overwise in material things, and drift away from the spiritual. It would be presumptuous in man to limit the power of God; the world in His hands is like a soap-bubble in man's; and can He who made the sun and moon give light, fail, if He so desired, to make the light on the inside, as the outside, of the world within and without, the soap-bubble?"

"Prophet of God," said Oratonga, "your views are so new, so wonderful, so incomprehensible, that I can neither accept nor reject them. Your prophets are wonderful men, and while they are specific about the future of Israel - can they give me no clue to the fate of the Chickimecs, and the Mound Builders?"

"Mortal," replied Melchisedec, "all mankind are His children. While our prophets mainly are inspired about Israel, the Lord sometimes teaches by the Urim and Thummim, the destiny of other nations. In yonder Tabernacle, in the Holy of Holies, our high-priest goes into the Holy of Holies once a year, barefooted, free from sin; clean within and without. In three days that event will come off, we are tarrying even now for it. Give me our passport through your dominion, come to the camp of Israel, and I'll make known to our high-priest your desire."

Oratonga ordered the passport to be made, which he received, and then Melchisedec returned to the Israelitish camp with the same composure with which he approached.

The passport read as follows:

1007

REBECCA.

1008

"In the field. Camp of Oratonga.

"The puissant, all-powerful Oratonga, Emperor of the Chickimecs, commands under penalty of death that safe conduct be granted to Melchisedec, king of Salem, and all the tribes of the children of Israel, women, children, Tabernacle, Ark of the Covenant, and all kinds of animals, property, arms, accoutrements, warlike implements, and all the belongings of every kind and character whatsoever; that all possible aid, protection, care, provisions and hospitality, be shown each one, and all of said Israelites, and any violence, insult, or want of courteous and hospitable treatment, shall be punished by instant death.

"In witness whereof I hereunto set my hand and insignia of power,

"ORATONGA, Emperor."

That the reader may better understand this chapter, we state that Oratonga was Emperor of the Chickimecs, and was at the head of a mighty army; that they were fighting to recover their native land from the Mound Builders, and, after ten years of desperate fighting, had pressed the Mound Builders out of Ohio and Indiana, as this territory is known in modern geography. Oratonga was encamped near the boundary-line of Indiana and Illinois, where this chapter is located. A full history of this conflict can be found in a volume by the author of this work. Oratonga was naturally solicitous to learn the result. He was superstitious enough after what he had seen, and heard from Melchisedec, to learn what the high-priest might divulge after looking behind the veil of futurity, in the Ark of the Covenant.

CHAPTER II.

NARDO AND REBECCA.

AFTER THE interview between Melchisedec and Oratonga, frequent interchanges of visits were had, and no one was more cordially received among the Hebrews than the young and talented Nardo. From the report of Melchisedec, it was known that Nardo was the first to recognize the mediatorial power of Melchisedec, and he was everywhere welcomed as a visitor to the Israelitish camp.

While he was filled with wonder at the Tabernacle, the cloud above it, the grave and austere appearance of the priests, the sacrifices, the daily prayer at the call of the trumpet, the regular and systematic arrangement of the tribes, their cheerfulness, temperance, and good deportment, it was not long before he noticed a dark-eyed beauty, in the tribe of Simeon, located at the southwest corner of the encampment. Her black abundant hair fell in wild luxuriance down her neck and shoulders. Her eyes, large, dark as midnight, fringed with long lashes, and rendered beautiful by exquisitely-arched eyebrows, gave a deep and brilliant aspect to the mellowed and serene appearance which softened her otherwise keen and penetrating glance. Her nose was straight, a departure from the Jewish to the Grecian type, full lips suggesting love and sweetness. Her whole countenance indicated strength, nobility, and intelligence much above the average, and while being conducted around the camp, Nardo suddenly encountered Rebecca. Her large expressive eyes, her open countenance, the mingled dignity, sweetness, and nobility of her appearance, made a deep and powerful impression upon him. His eyes seemed fascinated by hers, and both gazed upon the other with a look that seemed to cling and fuse, and melt in and make them recognize each other as congenial souls.

As a poet has expressed it:

"So came thy every glance and tone,
 When first on me they breathed and shone,
 New, as if brought from other spheres,
 Yet welcomed as if loved for years."

Rebecca recovered first, and when Nardo was introduced, she greeted him so graciously and was so self-possessed that his admiration was further increased.

He lingered longer at Simeon's headquarters than at

1010

any other, and before leaving was invited to come again; and when he left, he bore away a sprig of evergreen, given him by the enchanting Rebecca. He went the rounds of all the tribes, but he carried a remembrance of Rebecca, which he could not well shake off, and, in fact, did not desire to do so.

The next time he called he found her making a garland of flowers to bind around her classical head, and Nardo said:

"Fair Jewess, I have somewhere heard it said that flowers are 'the smile of God,' and certainly there is nothing lovelier, sweeter, more delicate; and it is a tradition among our people, that when the earth was young, in the early days of creation, things were coarser, and gradually refined themselves; that then flowers were unknown upon the earth until one appeared who was considered to be an angel, with bunches of flowers, which were planted and grew vigorously, and the supposed angel turned out to be a woman. Thus God's best gifts to man were woman and flowers."

"Oh, brave and gallant Chickimec," said Rebecca, "your statement is both new and flattering to me. I never heard before that woman had a celestial origin above that of man, but I can well believe that the beauty and fragrance of flowers give us one of our purest and most refined pleasures. If there is in nature anything which refines by their subtle and sweet influence, it is flowers. They teach our race a duty by keeping before our eyes their sweetness, and thereby appealing to the delicate and beautiful in us. Wheresoever they bloom they are constant reminders of how good and sweet and pure we may be if we have their modesty and loveliness. It has been said that for man's misfortune at Eden, 'some flowers blush white as sea-beaten shells, and some are always blushing.' Certain it is that man and woman in all ages use them as talismans of their best and truest affections, and I doubt not that our heavenly Father has sent them here as reminders of the glories of the Hereafter. It may be as you say, 'the flowers are the smile of God,' scattered upon the earth, if so they will strengthen our faith in Him and teach us that mankind has faith in Him and teach us that mankind has something of the celestial in him, and cause us to look upward with a more trusting faith."

"Yes, yes," said Nardo, "they make us look up. They teach us that the bird, which sails above the cloud, and is nearest to heaven, is safest 'from the fowler's snare,' and so when we keep our eyes and minds on justice, purity, and duty, we ascend nearer to the skies, and are safer from the temptations of sin and the allurements of earth."

"I see the beauty and significance of all you say," replied Rebecca, "but you must remember while our thoughts can mount higher than the eagle, with his eye on the sun, that our bodies are still on the earth, and faith is like the needle which points to the north, where we are going; we are tossed on the billows of life's tempestuous sea, and we need, like the beautiful flowers, to be sweet, and pure, in all daily thoughts, to escape the snares of earth, and the weakness of the flesh; and as the needle points to the north, our faith must never falter, but reach upwards like yonder cloud," and Rebecca pointed with her shapely hand towards the cloud that rose over the tabernacle and pierced the skies.

"You are correct," rejoined Nardo. "When the waters of a clear and placid lake are sleeping in tranquillity, they mirror each passing bird, each floating cloud, and the heavenly blue of the fathomless sky; but when the winds blow, and the storm comes, they throw up mire and clay; it therefore behooves us to look well to ourselves, when the storms of sin and temptation overtake us, and beat through our skies."

"You talk like a philosopher, and as wise as some of our prophets" said Rebecca, "but faith after all is the simplest and easiest thing, when rightly understood. An elder in Israel once asked a child, 'what faith was,' and the reply came, 'taking God at His word, and asking no questions.' An Israelite was once captured by a heathen king and was sentenced to death, and the sword was raised to behead him, when, oppressed with an intolerable thirst, he asked for water. A cup was handed to him, and the king said, 'You can live until you have drunk that water!' The cup was

1012

THE HIDDEN WORLD

instantly dashed to the ground, and the condemned man said, 'A king never goes back on his word.' And thus his life was saved."

"Israelitish woman, I will venture to tell you in confidence, what no other person has ever been told, and what I will tell for I have confidence in you, and I feel certain that you can understand it, and you will see that I take God at His word, as your captive did the heathen king. I had always been a believer in God, for it seemed to me that if one was like the ox, or swine, that would lay down in clover or wallow in the mire, and have no conception of a God, they deserved a like destiny, annihilation. And through our land there came, years ago, an Israelite, who said Abraham was his father and Christ his Saviour, and he taught such a beautiful theory, that I was deeply impressed. He claimed that common people called Christ a prophet, but his disciples called him the Son of God. That He cured the blind, raised the dead, walked on the water, calmed the tempest, abated the winds, silenced the thunder, chained the lightning, cast out demons, and worked miracles, showing dominion over the elements, man, and evil spirits, and worked out wonderful miracles, such as omnipotence only could do. That He had the most commanding personality, His face was unwrinkled, was smooth as marble, and His pale, olive complexion had a lovely tint of red and white like the blush where the white of the sea-shell blends with the pink; His look innocent, gentle, yet commanding, that men in His presence had their feet often rooted to the ground; His conversation full of parables; courteous, grave, and all-persuading, but terrible in reproof. Thousands have seen Him weep, none ever saw Him smile; He was a man of grief, not for Himself, for He was sinless, modest, bold, wise, merciful, forgiving; He was of surpassing loveliness; was crucified, arose the third day, and is now in heaven, interceding for mercy and forgiveness for all humankind, that all who should call upon Him would inherit everlasting life. While I was always willing to worship God, it seemed to me that to acknowledge Christ as my Saviour would be an insult to God. That to worship other than God would be

1013

wrong, that the worship should be to God, and not to a subordinate, and for a long time I was in doubt, was extremely unhappy, miserable; for the Spirit was at work in me; it seemed as if some terrible calamity was to overtake me, my heart ached, my soul was sick, and I could almost hear in the sky and air around me the adumbration of a coming doom. My suffering was indescribable, because it was the torment of the spirit, and not the flesh. This good man was holding meetings, proselyting for Christ, preaching Him to a dying world, and, finally, I became so desperate and miserable that I concluded, as a last resort, to throw myself into the arms of Christ, and take Him at His word.

"I went home, I retired, and thought it all over, feeling as miserable as a man could, having a consciousness that I was a sinner and under condemantion. Then I recalled the fact that I had not accepted Christ unconditionally, only on the ground that if He gave me relief I would accept Him wholly and without any mental reservation, but if I found no relief I would reject Him and fall back on God.

"And so I mentally promised, before going to sleep, to take Christ as my Saviour, and rely upon Him wholly, considering that if it was God's plan to have a mediator, I would not criticise but accept Christ. Soon my aching heart found such relief that I went to sleep, and how long I slept I cannot tell, but I suddenly awoke one of the happiest of men on the earth.

"If it is possible for a man to be happier than I was, it could only be in heaven and under the eye of God.

"I was enveloped and completely surrounded by a bright light as of electricity, but softer and of exquisite loveliness. Successive waves of delicious healing, purifying currents, swept over me, apparently cleansing my heart, and I felt as if dark, black scales were being loosened, and flowing away and passing out of my person, and every successive wave swept away the black corroded scales of sin and filth, and this continued until finally my heart, much smaller, but cleaned, purified, and white as alabaster, was full of unspeakable happiness, and I felt thoroughly cleansed of the

1014

Adamic and personal sins.

"What was strange, I could see and feel these successive waves as they swept down over and purified my heart.

"I felt then that I knew my Redeemer liveth, that I knew what a new heart was, that I knew what a new birth was, what the Holy Spirit was. The new birth and the new heart were no longer a mystery; it was a spiritual and not a birth of the flesh. And I knew what transcendental, indescribable and unspeakable happiness was. And, more than that, I caught a faint idea of Christ's love, and it has been transplanted into me, for I have an all-embracing love. I love all things, for they are from God's hands. I see nothing but I love it, for I carry love and heaven around in my new heart.

"I love and pity the vilest sinner. I pity him, because he cannot see and love God as I do, and the element of hate is forever eliminated from my nature, and I cannot hate any one. If one does me wrong, I love him still, for God made him, and I love all from God's hand. He is in the gall and bitterness of sin, and under the curse of sin, that fell on Adam at his transgression, as I was, and the poor fellow is under the cloud.

"But I am in the sunlight and under the care and marvelous protection and peace of God. I love the birds, the flowers, the clouds, the earth, the sparkling rivulet, the placid or stormy lake, the rolling ocean, the glittering stars, the smallest bug that creeps or the gnat that flies; to be brief, I love all I see, feel, smell, hear, touch, or comprehend, for God made them; and I cannot hate anything, but love and pity all things for His sake, and because they are His handiwork, and He has pronounced them 'good.'

"And this brings me to the point of faith, displayed by the Israelitish captive to the heathen king. And now that is my faith. And whether you or any other person doubt my assurance, let me say, Jewish maiden, nothing on earth, nothing under the earth, nothing within the earth, no argument of man, no beclouding philosophy, no carping agnostic, no unbelieving atheist, no deceiving devil, no misleading spiritualist will ever shake my faith in Christ. Provided always the good Lord gives me a memory of the past and a sound mind."

"Brave Chickimec, I have never heard an experience like yours. It has around it the halo of heaven, you have tasted of the unseen manna from the gardens of God. I would not if I could question your faith, for it is like that of Abraham. Our people are now and have for generations looked for a Messiah, who possessed the attributes of Him you call Christ. He is rejected of our people, because as we see it some of the prophesies have not yet been fulfilled. While I tacitly acquiesce in what they teach and believe, still the Christ you acknowledge is such a worker of wonders and miracles, that I confess I am sometimes staggered, and at nothing so much as your wonderful experience as a Gentile, and while I thought my faith adamantine, permit me to say that I have not encountered among our people a faith so sublime as yours, except in our grand prophet Melchisedec; and it seems to me a faith like yours should belong to the Hebrew nation."

"Fair Jewess, you are right, and it is even so in fact, and not in form. The man whose preaching converted me was a Hebrew, and so if not by actual physical at least by spiritual adoption, I am a Hebrew, and when I saw Ten Osta and the Alatongas perish, I knew Melchisedec had a hold on heaven, and I formed a resolution to join your people, if the thing is possible."

"Brave and wise Chickimec, our people have always adopted those whom we call heathens, and by the word we mean no disrespect, but it is a term meaning all other people except our own, and I am sure you would be thrice welcome, as I learn you seem to understand all languages, almost as well as your mother-tongue, and your services would be invaluable in our travel northward, to the end of the world, or into it, for we are to be hidden in it until the Messiah comes, until the dead are raised, until the third temple is built, never to be destroyed as our prophet Zechariah declares in the thirteenth chapter and ninth verse where he says:

" 'And I will bring the third part through fire, and will refine them as silver is refined, and I will try them as gold

1016

is tried: they shall call upon my name, and I will hear them: I will say it is my people, and they shall say, The Lord is my God.'"

"And when you do join our people, and I hope with all my heart you will, that you will join the Tribe of Simeon, so we may journey northward in the same tribe."

"Fair Jewess, your slightest wish would be imperative law to me, and your elevated character and religious sentiments will strengthen my faith in God, and it shall be with the Tribe of Simeon, and no other.

"I have been taught that the first face we see is a mother's, beaming with love, the last we behold is that of a sympathetic friend, and that the face which gives us the most happiness or sorrow is the one we see between the first and the last," and Nardo looked directly into the glowing countenance of the Jewish maiden.

Rebecca hesitated for a second, and while her dark eye took on a deeper and more glorious look than Nardo had ever seen before, she rallied and said, archly:

"There is but one face altogether beautiful, that of a follower of God, and if we live a pure life, the soul within will shine out sweet and as lovely as these flowers; and as a type and a shadow, as we Jews so often say, of a new, but I trust a durable friendship, accept these buds; I gathered them from a rose-bush I brought from Sharon."

Nardo, was for a moment speechless with surprise and pleasure, but he gladly accepted them, and then said:

"Rebecca, excuse me for calling you Rebecca, I will accept these buds, and I will put the construction upon them most pleasing to me, and, if you do not object, that which custom and the interpretation of mankind allows."

With woman's quick comprehension and tact for emergencies like the present one, Rebecca said:

"Without discussing the world's interpretation concerning flowers, there is a deeper one concerning the condition of man after death.

"Since we have interchanged ideas so freely, I shall not hesitate to express myself as to the ultimate fate of man, and of Israel in particular. Understand, I am not claiming that these are Hebrew ideas, and orthodox, and I give them simply as mine. As I understand the prophets, Satan is to have power over evil-disposed persons, for a definite period of time, long enough to show man's proneness to evil, and his powerlessness to save himself, and the necessity of a Saviour, and this will continue until Israel returns to Jerusalem. Then the city of God will descend upon the earth. Through the center shall flow a pure river of crystal water, flowing from the throne of God, along which is the Tree of Life, with fruit for the immortals to eat, where there is no sun, for the Lord shall give them light. Satan shall gather his mighty army of the unbelieving, abominable murderers, whoremongers, sorcerers, idolaters and all liars, and encompass the city, when God shall send His fire and destroy Satan and all his followers. This will be the end of evil, when 'righteousness and peace shall cover the earth as waters cover the sea.' Then shall come the new earth and the new heavens, and from one new moon to another, and from one Sabbath to another, shall all flesh come to worship before God."

Nardo was transfixed for a moment by these wonderful words, but recovering himself said:

"Rebecca! Wise Jewess! I am at a loss which to admire most, the felicity of your language or the splendor of the scene you describe. You speak like a prophetess! I now see, as never before, the wisdom, justice, power, and mercy of God. In suffering Satan to have dominion over man, whom he deceived, for a season, He was wise in letting man suffer for disobedience, He displayed His power in bringing the city of God to the earth, in destroying Satan and ending his opportunity to deceive at one blow, and crowning it all with His mercy in sending Christ to redeem man from the thraldom of death, and the dominion of sin. What a spectacle of transcendent splendor, far-reaching glory, and omnipotent mercy! 'A pure river of water, clear as crystal, running through the city, with the Trees of Life along for fourteen hundred and sixty miles of golden streets, the people going up once a month, eating the fruit and drinking the crystal waters of life, thus re-

1018

newing themselves in beauty and strength for that immortal life intended when Adam and Eve were placed in the garden of Eden."

"Yes," said Rebecca, "this vision is often before me, and you can more clearly see why we are sent out of a sin-sick world, to be separated from, and not to be counted among the nations, and why we are to be hidden in its interior until called to Jerusalem, in the fullness of time."

"Precisely so," said Nardo. "And imperial justice terminates Satan's reign, infinite mercy surrounds man, and God's eternal plan is carried out, and the earth made the most glorious of all the constellations of the sky, because it has been purchased by the blood of Christ, and made pure and incorruptible by omnipotent power.

At this moment a blast of a trumpet was heard, a sound of martial music, and Oratonga and his principal officers were seen approaching the encampment; and we must now turn our attention to other matters, and leave Nardo and Rebecca to the imagination of the reader, for all can see - that -

"Love took up the glass of time, and turned it in his glowing hands,
Every moment, lightly shaken, ran itself in golden sands."

CHAPTER III.

THE TABERNACLE - THE FATE OF TEN OSTA.

THE regular encampment of the Tribes, their separation and yet perfect capacity for union, each tribe having a flag, and all surrounding the tabernacle, struck the practiced eye of Oratonga as the most perfect arrangement he had ever seen. But what most impressed him was, the court and the tabernacle. The court was seventy-five by one hundred and fifty feet. Sixty pillars of dark black acacia, seven and a-half feet high, and seven feet apart, made the frame-work. Each pillar rested on copper sills, held in position by cords connected with pins driven in the ground, and had capitals

1019

plated with silver. Silver rods ran from one capital to another, and from these rods silver hooks were suspended, to which curtains of fine, pure linen, snowy white, hid the inside of the court. At the eastern end of the court were four entrances, in all thirty feet wide, and curtains were sometimes lifted, and one could then look into the court and see the brazen altar, or the altar of burnt-offerings, situated between the entrance of the court and the tabernacle.

An incline of earth led up to one side of the altar where a platform entirely surrounded it. The four corners of the altar were ornamented with horns where the innocent were sheltered, where man-slayers fled for safety, until properly tried.

Beyond the brazen altar was a layer of brass, standing on a pedestal, where the priests washed their hands and feet whenever they entered the sanctuary.

At this moment a wild, sweet sound of many musical instruments smote the air, and a line of priests, singers, and musicians, appeared to conduct the high-priest into the court, and to the entrance of the tabernacle.

The Levites made prayer to the Lord with musical instruments as follows: "Praise Him with the sound of the trumpet; praise Him with psaltery and harp; praise Him with timbrel and dance; praise Him upon the loud cymbals; let everything praise ye the Lord." - Ps. cl. 3, 4, 5, 6.

Oratonga was seated with Melchisedec on a platform overlooking the court, where he could see the entire proceedings. After the procession arrived near the altar, a high-priest emerged from the holy place or sanctuary, and advanced beyond the layer, and meeting the head of the procession they halted, and the high-priest placed his hand on the neck of the tame and beautiful animal selected for the sacrifice, and invoked the mercy of the Lord, and asked His acceptance of the sacrifice for Israel, and all friendly nations."

And this is the spectacle which Oratonga witnessed, and it was the first time heathen eyes had ever seen the same in America. While the animal was slain, cut up and burned, and the customary services were being performed, Oraton-

1020

ga was eagerly scanning the tabernacle, and the wonderful cloud that rose straight up in the air, and disappeared beyond the reach of human vision.

While the priest and the sacrifice were new and strange to him there was something weird, mysterious, and sublime in that silent cloud. Its foot came down within a short distance of the blue top of the tabernacle, and then rose like an arrow, of the same symmetrical size, straight up, piercing the sky, reaching above the clouds of earth, which swept and floated by, but away above them it pierced the blue of the heavens, as if it might reach eternity itself.

Birds were passing far below the clouds of earth, and occasionally flew behind this cloud, and disappeared for a time, but, there it was, towering above birds and clouds, and as Oratonga's eyes swept up towards the fathomless blue, he shrunk within himself, and felt what a helpless being man was; and while he was at the head of a mighty army, and emperor of millions of Chickimecs, yet what was he in comparison to the omnipresent Creator of all? And he could not well shake off the powerful impression of that mysterious cloud.

Observing the wrapped attention of Oratonga, and defining somewhat that was in his mind, Melchisedec spoke and said:

"Yonder cloud, in the days of Moses, did not rise so high. But since our journey across Europe and Atlantis, it has reached beyond human vision, and when we passed through the five large countries of Atlantis mentioned by Plato, the sight of this cloud has been our passport, and it will be our guide until we enter into that Northland, where we shall remain, hid from the world, until Israel returns to Jerusalem."

"Prophet of Israel, that cloud would have been sufficient for me, but for Ten Osta and the Altongas, they must first perish before conviction. And even now, there are some doubters, growlers, and malcontents who claim there is some chicanery or deception, and I have with me yonder, the brother of Ten Osta, who sullenly contends against the evidence of his own eyes, and the absence of his brother,

1021

THE HIDDEN WORLD

and the disappearance of the Altongas, that there is some sham in the whole matter, and I have permitted him to come along today, hoping he may be cured of his misbelief."

"Such men never change," replied Melchisedec. "Their pride of opinion, and mystifying philosophy, keeps them in error; like plants under a shade they never bloom into spiritual life, always scientific, material, philosophical - once an atheist, always so."

At this moment the high-priest entered the sanctuary and lighted the altar of incense, and the slowly-parted curtains disclosed the miraculous light shining from around the cherubims, then the curtain of the tabernacle ran down, and Oratonga could see no more into the tabernacle. His quick eye noted a strange light of a reddish yellow and white tint, which hung around the cherubims, whose wing extended over the mercy seat.

Oratonga was told by Melchisedec, that "the high-priest would learn the will of God, concerning Israel, for the next year. Also that the priest had been requested to see, if it was to be revealed, what was to be the end of the conflict between himself and the Mound Builders.

Meanwhile, now that the sacrifice was over, and the curtain drawn in front of the tabernacle, Oratonga addressed himself to an examination of that remarkable structure.

He could see that the walls were solid, on the north and south side, and open to the east, except that there were curtains, instead of solid walls. The walls were made of boards of black acacia wood, susceptible of high polish; how they were fastened at the top, he could not see.

"They were about fifteen feet high. The lower end rested on silver bases, they were massive blocks, weighing about eighty to ninety pounds, and mortised, and made a very solid foundation. The inner covering was of the finest and whitest linen, the most beautiful cloth then known. Interwoven therein were cherubims in threads of blue, purple, and scarlet. Over this beautiful covering was a curtain of goat's hair, black in color. The third covering was sheep's-skin, dyed in red, and dressed to look like morocco leather,

1022

shining and beautiful. The outer covering was badger skins, so colored as to be like the sky. Whether the tabernacle was blue, scarlet, white or black, depended on the weather, or how many coverings were in use at a given time." Of its interior structure, of its golden candlesticks, silver rods, silver rings, the posts, furniture, Ark, Mercy-seat, bowls and equipments, sheathed with gold, and inlaid and decorated with precious stones, Oratonga could not tell, by personal inspection, as he was dependent upon Melchisedec, for these matters, but he was told by him "that the Ark of the Covenant, and tabernacle disappeared from the Jewish world, and it was no wonder, for they were taken by the Ten Tribes, composing this encampment, and they disappeared so unexpectedly, and so completely, that they are called the 'Lost Tribes of Israel.' "

"The Tribes of Benjamin and Judah remained as a body with some of all the tribes, and constitute the Jews in the world, and will remain a distinct people, until they meet the so-called 'Lost Tribes,' when the Lord calls them all back to Jerusalem, at the restoration."

While this conversation was going on, they were suddenly interrupted by loud cries of rage and anger, and a Hebrew, hatless, with clothes in disarray, was seen coming at full speed, with terror depicted upon his countenance, and he plunged into the open space, which led into the court of the tabernacle, crying aloud as he came, "Refuge, refuge, make way to the horns of the altar." The few priests who lingered about the altar on which the sacrifice still was smoking, gave way to the frightened and panting fugitive, so he might reach the horns of the altar. A wild commotion and tumult was seen along the front of the tribes of Reuben, and Simeon, and Issachar. And behind the panting Hebrew, the brother of Ten Osta, bleeding from a spear-thrust, with raised battle-ax, and a face lit with diabolical passion was pursuing the fugitive. The Hebrew had dodged in and out among the tents of Reuben and Simeon, and had succeeded in outspeeding his ferocious pursuer.

"Impious dog and deceiver! Your people murdered Ten Osta, and I'll kill this Hebrew dog, if I run him into the

1023

cloud, and slay him in the teeth of your great Jehovah," and waving his battle-ax, he pressed onwards to the open way leading into the court.

Meantime the panting fugitive grasped the horns of the altar of burnt-offering and said: "Bless the Lord, saved!"

Just before the passionate Altonga reached the open way into the court, the curtain shot down suddenly before him. But it only increased his blind passion; he swung his battle-ax viciously at the swaying curtain, but it never reached the mark, his ax went hurling upwards, and the giant fell, limp and dead. He was thrown flat on his back, his arms extended, just in the attitude they were when he attempted to strike, and a most terrible and agonized expression was upon his countenance.

The line of pursuing Altongas, who had been following the giant, to give him support, halted with fear and dismay, and gazed upon the dead and awful face of the brother of Ten Osta. After the first benumbing terror wore off, they cautiously advanced to pick up his body, but were whirled round and round, and faced from the slain giant, and they hurriedly marched away, with faces as pale as the dead man's.

When Oratonga witnessed this mysterious and miraculous transaction, his blood grew cold, his face paled, and, turning towards Melchisedec, he said:

"Will they never learn anything?"

"Never," replied Melchisedec, "the minions of Abaddon, the unbelieving sons of perdition, doubt all things, except some dogma of misleading science, or the apparent perfection of human reason. But I must have the dead Altonga removed and carried to a place where his comrades may convey him back to your camp."

Melchisedec descended from the side of Oratonga and walked along slowly and reverently towards the prostrate man, whose stiff, extended arms were uplifted towards that Jehovah whom he had so recently defied.

Melchisedec kept his eyes upon the dropped curtain and when arriving near it lifted his hands and uttered a silent prayer, when the curtains rolled up, as suddenly as they

1024

THE HIDDEN WORLD

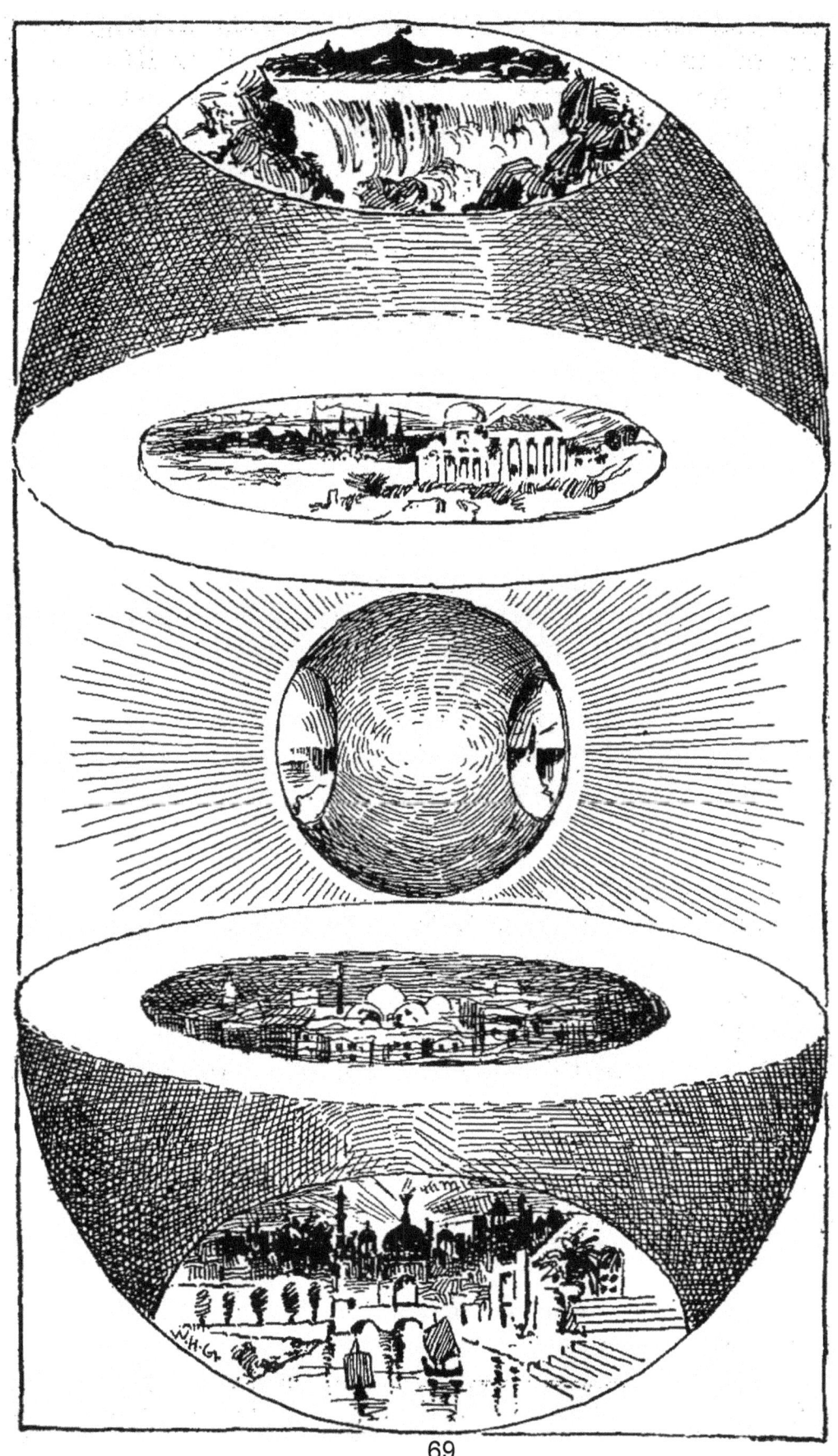

EARTH IN SECTIONS, SHOWING INNER WORLD.

THE HIDDEN WORLD

fell, and the fugitive Hebrew was seen, holding on to the horn of the altar. A wavering, unsteady light flickered over the brazen altar, and the little smoke that remained over the dying fire, raised, whirled slowly round and round, and gradually grew less and less, until it disappeared altogether, and the common sunshine, and the softly-blowing wind, proclaimed that Jehovah had withdrawn from the court, and it was safe once more for the passage of consecrated priests or fugitives from justice. Again

> "I falter where I firmly trod,
>   And falling with my weight of cares,
>   Upon the great world's altar-stairs,
> That slope thro' darkness up to God.
>
> "I stretch lame hands of faith, and grope,
>   And gather dust and chaff, and call,
>   To whom I feel is Lord of all,
> And faintly trust the larger hope."

When the slain giant was turned over to his comrades, they tried in vain to put his hands at his side; but they never succeeded. They tried every way to smooth the look of horror and fear upon his countenance; but it was in vain. His muscles were as hard as granite. They buried him with fear, and were glad when the friendly soil hid his distorted countenance. They could never obliterate from their memories his looks any more than they could smooth out the imprint of Jehovah's seal on his face, or lower the arms outstretched for that mercy which he refused to the fleeing Hebrew, and which the Lord of All refused to him. "As ye sow, so do ye reap."

CHAPTER IV.

A HOLLOW WORLD.

AFTER the events recorded in the last chapter, Oratonga and Melchisedec were waiting to hear what the high-
1026

priest might report, when Oratonga said: "I am desirous of knowing more concerning the religion of the Israelites, and why you are marching northward, toward eternal ice, snow, and frost."

"Emperor, at the head of all things, pervading every particle of matter, is a law called Force. Through this law mind acts, animals move, fire burns, winds blow, tornadoes rush, the clouds roll, the thunders boom, lightnings flash, earthquakes shake the ground, volcanoes erupt, and life and death coexist. There are in all things two fundamental essences: matter and spirit, and both are eternal, indestructible, and everlasting. Through force, matter and spirit are compounded, dissolved, and re-compounded, and out of this eternal change, in everlasting succession, man, and all organic life, is brought into existence. When Jehovah first commenced creation we know not, except as Moses, our great prophet, has told us; and through him we learn that the spirit in man is in some mysterious manner united with matter. Out of earth and spirit man was made, and he is to be eternal and immortal. And while the spirit is enshrined in the flesh, incarnadined in matter, both are subject to a law of the flesh and of the spirit, and all are subject to the law of our Lord and Creator, who kindly revealed Himself to Moses, and he has given it to us. And from what I have said you will see that all nations and people are of one blood, and are subject to the one law, because all are compounded alike out of matter and spirit, and all subservient to the same omnipotent force. And thus you see, in one sense, the Jew, and Chickimec, the Mound Builder, and Babylonian, Assyrian, and Egyptian, and all human beings, are all held by a common thread, like a strand through a lot of precious stones; and God has chosen our people to proclaim that there is but one Creator, the Lord God, the Great Jehovah, the I Am, that I Am. And this omnipotent Power is likewise omnipresent, and fills all creation; but since He has chosen our people, He manifests His presence to the common people and the heathen by yonder cloud by day and a pillar of fire by night. But to the priests He makes Himself known in the Holy of

Holies by the aid of the Urim and Thummim, and the miraculous light shining from the altar, and to His prophets by an irresistible impulse which compels them to speak and write. But see, there comes the high-priest, and we will now learn something concerning our destiny and perhaps something concerning yours.'

"But what have we here?" said Melchisedec as the priest put into his hands a rude drawing or rather drawings, intended no doubt to illustrate something connected with the destiny of the Ten Tribes, showing by these drawings that the earth was a hollow sphere, and not a solid body, as has ever been believed since it was found the world was round, and not flat.

In looking at the drawing handed to him by the priest, imperfect and rough as it appeared, Melchisedec saw that both poles were open, and land, mountains, ships, and strange cities were seen beyond the verge.

The first picture was of the world, showing one of the poles, the North Pole, with the sun greatly reduced, illustrating the rays of the sun shining into the earth, and ships sailing up the verge, and one descending into, and one fairly in the interior, and sailing on one of the interior seas.

The next drawing showed the world open at both ends, with pictures of strange cities seen dimly therein. At the right and left was a picture of the world cut into halves, showing the open poles and interior parts, with faint pictures of interior cities. Beyond the verge, or at the opening in the earth, where the world gradually turned in and made the globe a hollow cylinder, the oceans ran in and adhered to the inner rim of the convex side of the earth, just as they do on the concave side, evidently held by the same law which holds the oceans of the world where we live. And from the drawings it seemed that the Arctic ocean ran through on the inside of the earth and out at the south-end pole, making a circuit around and through the earth, and dividing, on the outside of the globe, by the lands of Europe, Asia, Africa, and the Americas, and thus making the oceans of the world, as shown on our maps.

THE HIDDEN WORLD

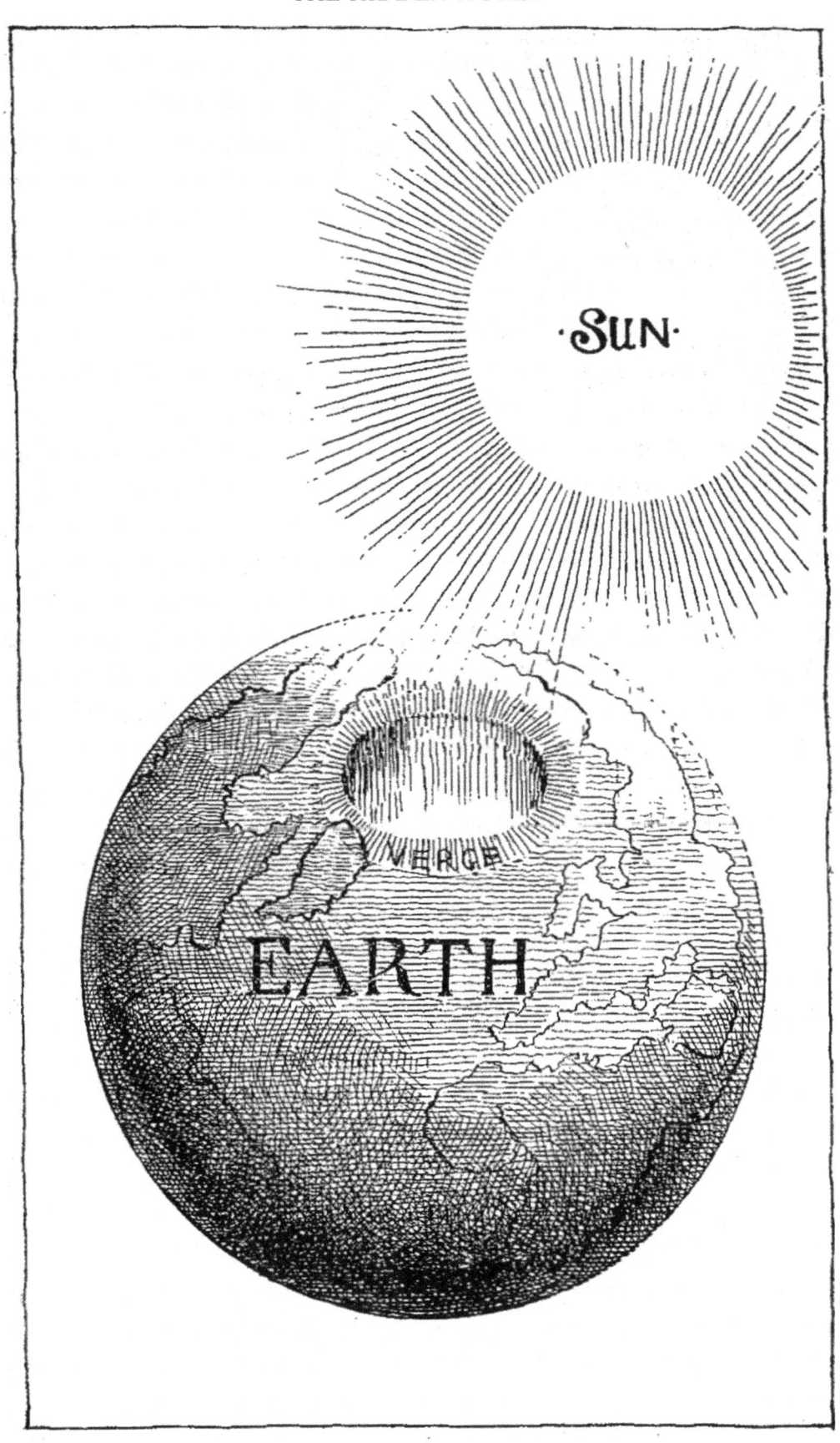

THE OPENING AT THE NORTH POLE, SHOWING VERGE AND SUN SHINING INTO IT.

THE HIDDEN WORLD

The next drawing was designed to show the various positions of the earth to the sun at the different seasons of the equinoxes, to show how the poles of the earth were enlightened at the spring, summer, autumn, and winter solstices; and by an examination it was seen that both poles are enlightened for six months, and two poles enlightened for the rest of the year.

After the first astonishment was over, Melchisedec said to the priest: "What does this mean?"

"It means simply that, in the vision which I beheld in the Holy of Holies, the Lord revealed to me the inner world, and I learned that in our journey northward we are to enter on the inner side of the sphere, and are to be hidden from the world until the fullness of time, and until Israel is called back from the Northland to Jerusalem. These are the pictures I drew. Examine them, and I feel by inspiration able to explain them as they appeared to me. I drew them as best I could. They are at your disposal."

Melchisedec took the drawings, and said: "I gather from these pictures some idea of what is intended; but, first, can you give me an idea of the probable thickness of the earth's crust?"

"About two thousand miles, but at the verges, about two thousand, five hundred miles," and the priest put his finger on the north and south ends of the picture, and then said, "about fifteen hundred miles at the equator, and gradually tapering north and south, to the two verges, to a thickness of two thousand five hundred miles, making a probable mean of two thousand miles thick."

"Well?" said Melchisedec.

"Taking the world to be eight thousand miles in diameter and the crust, varying between the equator, and the poles, or as you call it, the verges, from fifteen hundred to two thousand miles, the average of the two crusts would be four thousand miles."

"Exactly so," replied the priest.

"Then," said Melchisedec, "that would make a world on the inside of our globe of four thousand miles in diameter."

"Correct again, and it was revealed to me that this

1030

THE HIDDEN WORLD

inner world is not subject to the hurricanes, storms, heat, and cold, this bleak outer world is subject to - the magnetic storms of the sun, and the cold winds of the Arctic regions, and the hot equatorial blasts, which make our climate so variable and tempestuous."

Melchisedec said:

"I am not for a moment questioning what the Urim and Thummim discloses, but will you tell me why the water on the inside should not fall to the center of the inner world, and make it all a deluge of water?"

In justice to Melchisedec, be it said, he understood this, but the question was put for the benefit of Oratonga.

"I would not suppose," said the priest, "that a person of your intelligence, would ask such a question. You, of course, know the outside of our globe is round, and if I should ask you why does not all the water of the earth, when it turns round and under, if you will pardon the expression, run off, and drop we know not where, what would you say?"

"Oh," said Melchisedec, "it is the law of gravitation, which holds all to the surface of the earth."

"Very well, you have yourself answered your question. The same law of gravitation is on the outer and inner world, or rather crust of the earth. While the outer gravitation holds all firmly to the surface, the inner gravitation holds all to the inner crust of the sphere."

"See," said Melchisedec, "God's laws are immutable, and He who planned gravity, on the surface of the sphere, can place it likewise within the sphere. I can see if the crust of the earth is two thousand miles thick, that if a ball of iron should fall a hundred miles into the crust of the earth, every yard of its fall would decrease its speed, until it reached a point where the attraction of the inner crust equalized that of the outer, and the ball would come to a rest, being held in equilibrium by equal attractions, and I can now see how the water on the inside is held in position. Blessed be the name of the Lord!"

"Precisely so," said the priest, and if you were on the inside of the sphere, walking across a world four thousand miles around, you would not know that you were inside of

THE HIDDEN WORLD

a globe from anything your eyes could disclose, for man can see but a few miles at best. You could not see four thousand miles across, and as you traveled you would encounter hills, plains, mountains, islands, rivers, lakes, and oceans, just as you do in this world, and you would be in no more danger of falling in than you are of falling off, from this globe. The laws of gravity hold all in place, as the Creator has ordained."

"I see it, I see it!" exclaimed Melchisedec. "The Almighty God of Israel be praised! And were the world a solid sphere, continents could not sink, mountains could not rise or sink, whole continents could not fall in, for there would be no place to fall into a solid sphere; but will you please tell me what you mean by the verge, which I see marked on what we have always called the North and South poles."

"By the verge," replied the priest, "I mean that point for about fifteen hundred miles, where the north and south ends of the earth commence gradually to curve round and inward, and this is so gradual, that one could enter the interior of the world and be unconscious of its approach, by the use of his eyes, and his first astonishment would be to find his needle gradually dip, until it would finally point southward."

"Priest, that is a mystery to me, as we have always supposed that the needle pointed to the North Pole."

"There is no North Pole, but in its stead, an opening into the earth one thousand miles in circumference, and what we have supposed to be the North Pole is on the verge, where the thickest part of the crust is, and where the magnetic currents from the sun concentrate upon the verge, where the aurora borealis is, and there is where the true magnetic center is reached; and there is the real North Pole, and when that point is reached and passed, sailing inwardly, the needle will gradually turn downward, until it points south. You can see why this is so. The greater thickness of the earth, at the verge, converging together at that point, concentrates the attraction towards the largest mass of matter, and the attraction or gravity is there, and the magnetic currents from the sun focus at that point, and here is the ideal North Pole, which, after all, is but a fiction of science, and by vague conjecture located at a supposed frozen point at ninety degrees of north latitude."

To fortify the strange disclosures of the high-priest, made centuries before any travelers or hardy explorers ever attempted to discover the hidden secrets of the north part of the globe, a short disgression is made from the narrative to show what science and discovery have disclosed to confirm the mysterious disclosures of the Urim and Thummim in the hands of Israel's priest.

CHAPTER V.

THE TESTIMONY OF TRAVELERS AND EXPLORERS.

THE natural thread of our story is here broken to introduce scientific and historic evidence in support of the statements already made.

Captain Ross in his Explorations says, "That in high latitudes there are remarkable changes in the apparent extent of the visible horizon. From north to south the horizon is so limited, that objects can be seen only at very short distances, while in any direction, east or west, the horizon is greatly extended, and objects can be seen at an immense distance, as if upon a horizontal plane." "The direction north and south is directly over the convex surface of the globe, where the horizon is extremely limited, while along the surface of the verge, east and west, the view is along upon the plane of the verge, and the horizon is greatly extended. This is what would be as a result precisely from the existence of such a verge" (Symmes' Theory, p. 18). "Another beautiful phenomena observed by Captian Parry, is the elongated appearance of the sun and moon, in high latitudes, with the prismatic colors observed on these occasions. According to a simple law of optics, this is due to the dense atmosphere of the verges, acting like a prism, and causing the elongated appearance; and the prismatic

hues are due to the different refrangibility of the sun's rays."
"Captain Parry, and others, speak of the brilliant twilight of the north as being sufficient to enable them to read ordinary printed matter distinctly. This curious fact is wholly inexplicable upon the Newtonian theory of a solid globe, but is easy of explanation upon this. This twilight coming may be caused by the sun's rays thrown into the interior, through the southern opening, as shown by the opening in the South Pole, which, by two refractions, one at each opening, and two or three reflections from the inner concave surface would pass out at the north over the verge, and produce there this strange twilight. Captain Parry states when sailing northward in high latitudes, the North Star rises over the bow of the ship to the zenith, and then declines towards the stern."

"On the Newtonian theory the ship must sail directly under the North Star, and over and down upon the opposite side of the earth. But this cannot be true, for no navigator has sailed so far north. Further confirmation of a hollow earth is found in the variation in the dip of the magnetic needle." The line of the variation is over that part of the earth's surface where the needle points towards the largest part of the soil. But in the far north, above seventy to eighty degrees, the needle commences to fluctuate, so an author says: "The dip of the needle is nearly uniform upon the same latitude, but increases as the needle is carried north, and in high latitudes answering to the verge, the dip is greatly increased and becomes nearly perpendicular." The true magnetic poles are not at the points where the "line of variation terminates at the north and south, but are equidistant from this line immediately under the highest point of the verges north and south, and the line of no variation lies midway these magnetic poles. The needle, while it does not vary along the line to the right or left, yet as it goes northward or southward from the magnetic equator, it is attracted towards the true magnetic poles lying under the highest part of the verges, and so the dip is increased till it reaches the apex of the verge where it is greatest."

1034

THE HIDDEN WORLD

"The barometer also illustrates the theory; for it is well known that along the region of the verges, the mercury rises the highest, for the atmosphere is most dense there. It would be difficult to show upon any other hypothesis, why the barometer should rise higher along the locality of the verges, than upon the upper side of it north or south."

"The aurora borealis affords a most interesting illustration. Why is it exhibited always in high latitudes? The electric fluid pervades all nature, and is excited by heat, by cold, and by friction. The sun, in his daily course, rarefies the air of the equatorial region. It therefore rises and falls down towards the poles, causing currents from the equator towards the north and the south, where it is condensed. This process of rarefaction and condensation produces the aurora along the verges, where the greatest condensation takes place. In proof of this view, Captain Parry, and other explorers and navigators state that when in high latitudes "upon and beyond the verge, the aurora is almost always seen in a southwest direction." "Hearn found Indians, in latitude sixty, migrating west and northwest, seeking a milder climate on the approach of winter. Hearn, in 1789, traveled for a long time over a bleak, inhospitable country, and found it difficult to sustain existence. At length he found a milder climate sustaining vegetables, with forests of timber of various kinds, and animals different from any ever seen before," Captain Parry found "an Arctic sea, calm, clear, and free of ice, and warm-air currents coming from the north and northeast." Captain Parry, frequently mentions these warm currents. Large herds of deer, white bears, foxes, and other animals migrate northward, on the approach of winter. From regions around the northern part of the verges they migrated to the north, and from the southern border of the same they go south in the winter. The reindeer, in March or April, came down from the north in droves of thousands, and returned again in October in the interior of North America. In these latitudes, the musk-ox and white bear thus migrate. The cattle are seen retiring north on the ice in autumn, and returning in the spring in great numbers bringing their

1035

young with them."

"Immense shoals of herrings in good condition, according to Buffon, come down from the polar seas and are never known to return. They make the annual circuit of the earth, over the exterior surface and through both openings of the poles." (so called). "Driftwood is found in great quantities upon the northern coast of Iceland, Norway, and Spitzbergen. Vegetables of singular character, and flowers of peculiar fragrance and color unknown to botanists are sometimes in the drift."

"Hearn also informs us that swans, geese, brants, ducks, and other wild waterfowl are so numerous about Hudson's Bay in the spring and summer, that the company every season salt vast quantities of them, sometimes sixty or seventy hogshead. He enumerates ten different species of geese, several of which (particularly the snow geese, the blue geese, brant geese, and horned wavey) lay eggs and raise their young in some country unknown even to the Indians, as their eggs and young are never seen by them, neither have the most accurate observers been able to discover where they make their winter residence, as it is well known that they do not migrate to the southward, but few of them ever pass to the south, and some of the species are said never to have been seen south of latitude fifty-nine degrees." See Hearn's Journal, pp. 442,444,445, and 446. "As many as ten species of geese mentioned by Hearn never come south to winter, and in fact never come south at all. It seems clear that they raise their young beyond the icy circle, and within the sphere."

While the sensible horizon is far more extensive east and west, the elongated appearance of the sun and moon, the northern twilight, the apparent shifting of the north-star, the dip of the needle, the rise of the barometer, the aurora borealis, the milder climate, the warm northern currents of air, the migrating animals, the driftwood, the unknown flowers, all these unerring facts corroborate the disclosures of the high-priest: and right here I will cite the testimony of Archibald Stuart, published in the Indianapolis Daily Journal, which is in part a confirmation of what the

1036

Hebrew priest revealed so many centuries before. The article reads as follows.

IN THE FAR NORTH.

"Quebec, Aug. 11, 1894. Archibald Stuart, a young Scotchman of an adventurous turn of mind, who was visiting this city for sport, has just succeeded in doing what no white man before has done. With no other companion than his Indian guide, he has just completed in safety the trip from Lake St. John to Mistassini, the great mysterious inland sea in the far north, by one route and returning by another. He has brought back with him interesting accounts of legendary lore and tribal superstitions of the peculiar aborigines of this far northern country, and found very large areas of merchantable timber, and very large tracts of magnificent agricultural land in what was hitherto supposed to be nothing but a worthless wilderness."

We cite the following as the opinion of Floyd Hamblin, in the Utica Observer.

SYMMES' HOLE UP TO DATE.

That the crust of the earth is formed in layers no one will dispute, and that all substance on the surface of the earth is drawn by some force toward the earth's center is also undeniable. This is called centripetal force. To admit the existence of this force is equal to the admission of a counteracting force called centrifugal.

According to every experiment and all philosophical reasoning, there must be a line of equilibrium drawn somewhere between the center and the circumference of the earth. The exact location of this line will always be determined by the motion of the earth. It is on this line that the external and the internal forces meet in deadly conflict, striving for gravitatious power and the enforcement of their laws. The friction produced by these two forces must be the source of all internal heat and the eternal fire. It is these two opposing forces that form and sustain the im-

1037

mense balance-wheel called "the earth," which is 25,000 miles in circumference, but cannot exceed 200 miles in thickness, including the lava belt in the center.

The irregular motion of the earth will change the central line of gravity and cause an eruption of lava either external or internal. The earth when viewed as a whole is a unit, and so are the laws which operate it, whether applied to the external or the internal surface.

The law which reverses gravitation on this equalizing line has given us two earths in one, or a world within a world. The friction and heat of the earth at the equator are so much greater than they are at the poles that the law of electric equilibrium will produce an electric current to meet the demand for light and heat.

This internal earth is a counterpart of the external in all things, except that its Atlantic and Pacific are not quite so vast, and its Nile and its Amazon are not quite so long. Neither are its zones, its poles, or its equator, quite so high. Nature, with an impartial hand, has withheld no good thing from this new world that can be tasted of by any other. Humanity here is as far removed from Darwin as Darwin is removed from the chosen seed of Adam's race.

Who shall defy the ice-bound North and enter that "open sea" so long sought for and greet their long-lost cousins who migrated from Babylon 3,000 years ago?

And while it is unimportant whether the reader accepts or rejects these manifold proofs of the truth of what the high-priest disclosed, as a belief either way will not change a fact, for a fact, once clearly established, becomes immortal, and cannot be added to or diminished from, yet we have concluded to appeal to an astronomical theory to corroborate him. Among other evidences all persons have heard of the planet Saturn and his rings, a picture of which is given as an illustration of the hollow world.

It will be observed that the rings or rather the ring, nowhere adheres to the body of the planet; the ring is of the same material of the planet itself.

The appearance of Saturn proves that spheres, and at least one hollow planet, exists, and from that fact it is fair

1038

THE HIDDEN WORLD

to infer that other worlds are similar, unless we have proof to the contrary.

The planet Mars presents the same polar appearance as our earth. "The axis of Jupiter, is always at right angles with a line drawn to the earth, consequently his poles are never presented to us, but his belts which can be seen seem to speak loudly in favor of a plurality of spheres."

"Dr. Herschel has observed a faint illumination in the unenlightened part of the planet Venus, which he ascribes to some phosphoric quality in its atmosphere." See editor's note, to Adams' Philosophy, vol. 4, p. 204, Philadelphia, 1807.

"Query. Might not such an appearance be accounted for as rationally by supposing the rays of the sun to shine, or be reflected, through one of her polar openings, and to fall on the verge of the sphere at the opposite opening?"

We close the citation of authorities for this chapter by quoting from "The Popular Science Monthly," for September, 1894, published by D. Appleton & Co., 72 Fifth Avenue, New York City, wherein certain extracts are taken from the recent Annual Meeting of the Association of Ontario Land Survey, Canada. P. 655, reads thus: "A regular record of temperature was kept during the winter. Our thermometer was a standard spirit one, graduated to 62 degrees F., and had been tested at the Toronto Observatory. The record is on file in the Dominion Crown Land Office. On the 1st of November the temperature fell in a series of remarkably regular jumps - that is, there would be three days of cold, then a few days of slightly higher temperature, then another three days of cold, and so on, each drop being colder than the last. This went on with unbroken regularity until the third week in January, when it began to rise again in the same way, and with equal steadiness. On Christmas day the weather was beautiful, still, and cloudless, and the thermometer stood at zero."

Page 657. "Of the 2,200 miles, 850 was through an entirely new country, never before traveled by white men, and 500 miles was over the open sea of Hudson's Bay, at the very worst season of the year, between the middle of

1039

THE HIDDEN WORLD

September and the middle of October."

Page 660. "The traveler's stand in cold weather is tea, and men will do more hard work than they ever could accomplish on any form of spirit."

Page 662. "The same authority concludes, from various ascertained facts, that within the Arctic circle the summer mean increase as you get near the pole, and favors the theory of an open polar sea. It is certain that the pole of the greatest cold lies southward from Greenland among the western islands of the polar archipelago."

TESTIMONY OF THE STARS.

The world has yet only crossed the vestibule, to gaze in telescopic wonder at the celestial programme of the heavens. Castor show a green tinge in color, while others are red, yellow, violet and white. Pollux is said to be "a hundred times more luminous than the sun, while its nearest companion may be a body smaller than our planet Jupiter, but shining with its own light." Some stars are double, some triple, some quadruple, and some "glitter with interlacing rows of stars." Along the Pleiades there is a "narrow nebulous streak, along which five or six stars are strung like beads on a string." "In cluster 1360, as one sweeps over them with the telescope gradually towards the nucleus, I have often been reminded of the approach to such a city as London. Thicker and closer the twinkling points become, until at last, as the observer's eye follow the gorgeous lines of stars trending inwards, he seems to be entering the streets of a brilliantly-lighted metropolis." Figure 1532 shows a star in four parts, enclosed in three circles. See Garrett P. Serviss' article, and map, page 468, in the February "Popular Science Monthly" of 1895.

Serviss describes it thus:

"In the center glitters the star, and spread evenly around it was a circular nebulous disk, pale, yet sparkling and conspicuous. The disk was sharply bordered by a narrow black ring, and outside the ring the luminous haze of the nebula again appeared gradually fading towards the edge to

1040

THE HIDDEN WORLD

invisibility."

Here we have an outer ring, or nebula of white, a dark ring, and the star proper within the ring, or inner circle, and a white or nebulous light, on the outside of the star, a world of circles surpassing anything claimed in this work.

See pages 472, 473 and 474 of the same Monthly for the following:

"Such facts like these, connecting rows and groups of stars with mass and spiral lines of nebula, present terrible temptations to speculate; but who shall say that they do not also, like obscure signboards, indicate the opening of a way which, starting in an unexpected direction, nevertheless leads deep into the mysteries of the universe?"

The strange action of star 1295 suggests the idea of a catastrophe to Nova Aurigae, wherein Serviss says as follows:

"But what were the circumstances of the collision. Did an extinguished sun flying blindly through space plunge into a vast cloud of meteoric particles, and under the lashing impact of so many myriads of missiles, break into superficial incandescence, while the cosmical wrack through which it had driven, remained glowing with nebulous luminosity. Or was Vogal right when he suggested that Nova Aurigae could be accounted for by supposing that a wandering dark body had run into collision with a system of planets surrounding a decrepit sun (and therefore it is hoped uninhabited), and that these planets had been reduced to vapor and sent spinning by the encounter, the second outburst of light being caused by an outgoing planet of the system falling a prey to the vagabond destroyer. Or some may prefer the explanation based on the theory of Wilsing's that two great bodies, partially or wholly opaque and non-luminous at the surface, but liquid hot within, approached one another so closely that the tremendous strain of their tidal attraction burst their shells amid a blaze of spouting vapors."

It is evident that astronomers, philosophers, physicists, geographers, and geologists, are still in the dark, concerning the universe and the North and South poles, and the centre of the earth.

But we must no longer dwell on the evidence, pro or con, to establish or overthrow the Hebrew priest, but return to Melchisedec and Oratonga, and see what the Urim and Thummim may have disclosed concerning the fate of the Chickimecs, and the Mound Builders.

CHAPTER VI.

PROPHECY CONCERNING ORATONGA.

THE HIGH-PRIEST handed to Melchisedec a drawing, who, after a hasty glance at it, passed it to Oratonga, who looked at it steadfastly for a few moments and said: "Is this all you can tell about my destiny?" The high-priest replied:

"That is all, except I can give you some oracular explanation about the drawing. The animal at the left indicates great victory this side of the Misventura River.* (*Chickimec name for the Mississippi River.) The size of the horns indicates the greatness and splendor of the victories. Nothing can withstand the man who wears the red plumes such as you wear. This side of that river, and down to the Red River, the red plume will be irresistible. In the middle of the Red River, and running up to the mountains is the boundary line, which Jehovah fixed for the Chickimecs. That river and that boundary you cross at your peril. The boundaries and the duration of nations are fixed by Jehovah.

"You can see the black dots, along the center of the river. If you are wise you will never cross that line."

"Suppose," said Oratonga, who was displeased at the revelation concerning the crossing of Red River, "suppose the fortunes of war demanded a crossing of that river, what then?"

"Presumptuous mortal," replied the priest, "look at that," and he placed his finger on the picture of the red plume, flat on the ground, while the prostrate hat lay prone on the grass, surrounded by small mounds, "and upon that," and he put his finger upon the horns of the headless animal.

1042

"It is not for me to argue about the decrees of Jehovah," and the priest, with great dignity and composure, walked away.

Oratonga bit his lip, scowled, and was ill at ease, and while not skilled in the pictographic prophecy of the priest, he caught enough in the prostrate plume and the headless horns of the animal, and in the red plume and Red River, with its dotted lines, to fill his soul with overwhelming dread; but cautious and diplomatic as he was, he turned and said to Melchisedec with apparent assurance, but the fiber in his voice told how deep the words of the priest had sunk:

"Well, my friend, we must take life as it comes, we always hope that ultimate good will come out of present or prospective evil, that no one lives who treads the earth with aimless feet, and we can hope, that, somehow, good will come to all, and, whatever fate may befall the red plume or the black, I shall go wheresoever the star of destiny, or the apparent best interests of the Chickimecs may lead me. And while I confess some mystification in the picture the priest has given, I shall see that you are safely conducted through my empire towards that wonderful land beyond the icy regions of the north, or rather the verge; and as Nardo has been adopted into your faith by circumcision, I'll ask that, when you arrive at that wonderful Northland, you will permit him to return and tell us concerning it. But what is this I hear about the strange food, white as snow, which falls every few days, and that your people eat, and you rest one day and do no work therein."

"Emperor, that is manna. God fed our people on it for years, while in the wilderness. Since our separation from the tribes of Benjamin and Judah, and since we started for the Northland with the Tabernacle and the Ark of the Covenant, the manna has fallen once a week, and our people live on that during the Sabbath, as we did in the wilderness in Moses' time. It falls on every seventh day. On the night of the day preceding the Sabbath, our people gather sufficient to last over the Sabbath. It is white, about the size of coriander seed, it tastes like honey and wheat bread mixed, and has in it all the needed elements of food, and its eating

1043

keeps off fevers, cutaneous and malarious diseases, and leaves the stomach in a condition of perfect health. You can see how necessary it is to protect our people while passing through such a malarious country as this. It is to our people a weekly reminder of God's care, and we all look forward to the Sabbath with great interest, for our repast of manna."

"Prophet of God, the more I hear of your people and Jehovah, the more I wonder, admire, and am amazed. Can I see and partake of this wonderful manna?"

"No, indeed," replied Melchisedec, "you cannot eat it, you can see it on the ground, you can pick it up, handle it, but no heathen can eat it, unless he is circumcised and becomes a Hebrew, and a true one at that, for it one feigns to become a Few, but is not one in truth, heart, and soul, the manna corrupts between his hand and mouth, and we then disown him at once, and send him out to the world, as we send the scape-goat to the wilderness. Tomorrow morning, at sunrise, the ground will be white with it, come and see our people gather it."

"Can I bring any of my people with me?" asked Oratonga.

"Certainly, Jehovah will care for His people, and protect, as He has fed and guided them thus far."

Oratonga then left, but returned to his own people, pondering on all he had heard and seen, and resolved on the morrow to see the wonderful manna.

CHAPTER VII.

MANNA.

WHEN the first streaks of coming light shot their faint illuminations, like wavering phosphorescent beams, across the eastern sky, Oratonga and his bodyguard ascended the rolling slope of the prairie, west of the slumbering Israelites, and in silent expectation awaited the coming dawn.

The low, descending moon hung like a ball of light above the western and rolling slopes of the prairie. It was just setting, and the prairie grass shone like strands of silver along the top and in the line of its light. Just before the moon disappeared, the sharp nose and alert ears of a prairie-wolf on a distant ridge appeared into the waning and wavering light, its body advanced and shut out the last glow, and when the wolf passed, the moon was nearly gone, and for one short instant only, it flashed its vanishing rays on the tallest spears of grass, across which the brush of a wolf's tail was seen, as it mixed and mingled, and then all was dark, save that the stars held undisputed sway with night and the dawning day.

The glittering stars shone high over him, and when Oratonga lifted his eyes to the heavens, and saw their sparkling light and countless number, he was softened and touched by their magnificence, and he felt the littleness of man and the grandeur of God.

While they have no relation to our story, yet I will venture to quote some poetry about the stars, written thousands of years afterwards, and found in the "Autocrat of the Breakfast Table." The lines are quoted by the author simply to please himself, as they seem to him the sweetest conceit ever found by him in literature or tradition. I feel certain that if the brave Oratonga did not feel such an inspiration, while gazing on the sky, that every gentle woman and chivalric-hearted man, will excuse the writer for quoting the compact between the flowers and the stars, reading as follows:

"When Eve had led her lord away,
   When Cain had killed his brother,
The flowers and the stars, the poets say,
   Agreed with one another

To cheat the cunning tempter's art,
   And teach the race a duty,
By keeping on his wicked heart
   Their eyes of light and beauty.

A million sleeping lids, they say,
   Would be at least a warning,

1045

And so the flowers should watch by day,
  The stars from eve till morning.

On prairie, hill, dale, and lawn,
  Their dewy eyes upturning,
The flowers should watch from reddening dawn
  Till western skies are burning.

Alas, each hour of daylight tells
  A tale of shame so crushing,
That some turn white as sea-beat shells,
  And some are always blushing.

But when the patient stars looked down
  On all their light discovers,
The traitor's smile, the murderer's frown
  The lips of lying lovers,

They tried to hide their blushing eyes,
  And in the vain endeavor
We see them winking in the skies,
  And so they wink forever."

But to return, none can tell what mighty thoughts surged through the brain of Oratonga. He stood with folded arms, like Napoleon, when meditating about Jerusalem, the glory of Solomon, the dominion of Alexander, and dreamed of an empire surpassing all in the annals of history.

He was communing with nature, and he who thus communes leaves the confines of the flesh, and is audacious and seeks to discover the awful secrets of nature.

What to him is thunder-blast, or lightning's glare, the sunshine or the breeze? Untrammeled by the flesh, he goes in thought beyond every star in the wide arch of the sky; he heeds not the sailing cloud, the invisible wind tossing his red plume. In the wild sweep of the spirit it lifts him up, link by link, till he is oblivious of time and circumstances, - and so it was with Oratonga; and finally his eye fell upon the Dipper, and looking along the pivotal light, he saw the

1046

North Star, which hung over the north end of the world, where Melchisedec was going, and then imagination went out towards the mysterious crimsoned river, dotted with the marks of Jehovah's boundary line, the headpiece, the fallen horns, red plume lying among the mounds, the black plume waving erect, audacious and victorious. All was before him; a scowl was on his face, and in his profound meditation he failed to see the fast advancing dawn, until he was touched upon the arm slightly by an officer, who said:

"See, Emperor!"

Instantly he looked, and, lo, what a sight! The sun which rises suddenly from the prairie threw its morning beams upon a wonderful scene. Instead of lighting up waving grass and blooming flowers it shone on a land of snowy whiteness. All over the rolling swells, down their sloping sides, across the level plain, for a long distance around the Israelitish camp, the ground was of that color except where the prairie flowers lifted their lovely heads, and the contrast between their bright colors and the whiteness was enchanting.

No lovelier scene ever fell under mortal eyes. The hush of nature hallowed the scene. No living thing disturbed its silent and glistening beauty. Not even a bird flew across its serene whiteness. The rolling bluffs and swells seemed like cumulous clouds which had fallen softly and lightly from heaven. The rising sun, gleaming on each individual flake, made it sparkle like glittering diamonds under a midsummer sun. Overwhelmed with a scene so unexpected and of such transcendent beauty, Oratonga was silent, and his eye wandered to the Jewish camp. The tents of Israel, which looked last night so white and lovely, now appeared dull, lifeless, soiled and ugly; but the cloud which rose above the tabernacle had a supernatural clearness and a serenely radiant beauty which outshone the manna, for it pointed heavenward, and Oratonga, in his inmost soul thought to himself:

"The wonderful God of Israel!"

As if this silent monition of spiritual recognition had broken the spell of heavenly silence, a trumpet, clear, long

1047

and loud, sounded from the front of the tabernacle, and then an answering peal came from the tribe of Simeon, and then one from the other tribes, until all had responded. Over the wide camp, in a few moments, men, women and children poured out of all the tents, and commenced to gather manna, and all stopped when they had each gathered an omar which was enough to last through the Sabbath.

It took but a short time to collect all that was needed.

The manna was so plentiful that it was rapidly gathered.

Within a hundred feet of Oratonga, it lay thick and beautiful.

By his direction some was gathered and handed to him.

It looked exceedingly inviting, and as he turned it over in his hand, forgetful of what Melchisedec had said, he put some towards his mouth. Suddenly he smelled a nauseating stench.

He lowered his hand and a disgusting worm was in his grasp which immediately putrified. He threw the nauseating thing away, and he discovered others doing the same, and they all involuntarily drew away from the line of manna.

Oratonga spoke, saying:

"Melchisedec informed me no heathen could eat, but could handle, the manna."

He remained where he was, absorbed in wonder, until suddenly the manna disappeared, and the waving grass and prairie flowers assumed their usual appearance, and nature looked as if no miracle had been performed.

When Oratonga entered the camp, every Hebrew had an omar full of the beautiful and toothsome manna.

CHAPTER VIII.
DEPARTURE - NEWTONIAN AND CONCENTRIC THEORIES.

THREE weeks after the transaction concerning the manna, the Israelites broke camp, and started after the cloud, and it was the last that Oratonga ever saw of the cloud or that wonderful people. And, before we follow them in their journey, we turn aside to quote from the following

1048

THE HIDDEN WORLD

authors, as the events we are compelled to record are so variant from the common opinions of mankind concerning the North Pole and an arctic climate, that one's credulity is severely tested, and the records of modern days are needed to even induce one to read these events with any patience.

So deeply has the Newtonian theory about a solid globe, and so universally have maps and geography educated the public mind to regard the North Pole as a reality and everlasting ice as surrounding it, that he is considered visionary who holds that the earth is a hollow sphere and that a warm open sea is flowing where everlasting ice is supposed to hold her frosty dominion.

An arctic climate, a north pole under the north star, the aurora borealis, a magnetic needle pointing eternally to the north, are so firmly fixed in the public mind, that it will not tolerate one who questions these fixed and fundamental facts of science.

To assert that an open polar sea, a warm climate, currents of warm air blowing south, plants and animals flourishing, and flowers blooming beyond the verge, and the magnetic needle turning downwards, and the north star appearing over the stern of ships headed north, seem so incredible, that some impatient reader will feel inclined to relegate the author of this book to the limbo of a visionary, and as a pure act of self-defense I cite the following respectable authors and navigators to sustain, so far as their testimony may go to corroborate, his narrative.

No one who has not considered that it is barely possible that an icy verge may not trend around the earth, north and south, above eighty degrees of latitude and down to the sixtieth degree, that being the coldest region of the earth, where almost eternal winter reigns, and that as you go north or south of that, you will find it getting warmer and warmer until you arrive at the equator, on the outer crust, and at the center of the earth, the other way along its interior crust.

To many such a belief would seem preposterous.

Well, I hope such persons will carefully read what the

1049

following explorers, and northern navigators say, who are supposed to give veracious narratives of what they saw and experienced, and let it go for what it is worth. In passing it would be well to remember that many of these witnesses are men of veracity, many of them renowned for learning, some of them scientific men, botanists, geologist, and learned men of the highest standing and repute, and in some instances, men selected by their respective governments to lead voyages of discovery, in the interest of science and geography. And, what I cite, much of it is to be found in official reports, in many instances, to their respective governments.

Norpensjould, of Sweden, made a visit to the extreme North, and he tells as follows:

"It is impossible to find continents of ice south of eighty degrees of north latitude. That is, after passing the eightieth degree or magnetic pole, North, his compass indicated South as the direction we familiarly term North. . . . After passing this magnetic pole he found a timber country, large rivers, and an abundance of animal life. He was the first to make a north-east passage."

"An English explorer, Capt. Wiggins, after passing 80 degrees, found the country seen by Norpensjould. He made the acquaintance of the inhabitants whom he discovered spoke Hebrew. An account of his trip was published in the London Times, February 5, 1881. A Mr. Seebohm, who accompanied the expedition, took a ride on horseback, with several others, through this new country, and after his return to London he read a description of what he had seen before the Society of Arts, on John Street, Adelphi, with Mr. Clements R. Markham, C.B., F.R.G.S., F.S., F.S.A., in the chair.

"Mr. Seebohm and his party hired horses, at a half-penny a mile, and in their travels they saw flax, and quantities of wheat, selling at sixpence a pool of 40 pounds. Beef sold at one penny a pound, and other products at equally low prices. The country was rich in iron ore, as pieces picked up haphazard were so highly magnetic as to lift a large needle. There were copper mines, and ten or

1050

twelve gold mines, that yielded each from five to seven tons a year. The large trees would compare favorably with those of California. Among other products of which this fertile country boasts, may be mentioned wool, tallow, mammoth ivory, sable, ermine, squirrel, red, white, and blue fox, bear, otter, and lynx. Further south elk was found, and in one warehouse alone he saw more than a thousand skins." S.T. 66.

Captain Wiggins was then called upon by the Chairman to make some remarks. He said, "in addition to the mineral wealth already mentioned, he had found a fine quality of graphite. The animals he noticed were larger than varieties of the same species here. The inhabitants were tall, and spoke Hebrew, they had dark hair and complexions, and Roman noses. Would it not be logical to think that this was one of the lost tribes of Israel, for we read in the Bible "that they went up the Euphrates to the North, and dwelt in a land where man never dwelt before"?

Another explorer, who visited this new country, is Captain Tuttle, an old United States whaling master. He gives a similar account of the people, and says "they speak Hebrew." He found them well-contented and intelligent. He discovered during twenty-eight years' experience in the north, that every fourth winter was milder, and during one of these seasons he discovered this new country, which he says can only be reached with a steam vessel, as the current in Robeson's channel runs south at the rate of four to six miles per hour.

All of these discoveries were made while running south, above the 80 degrees of north latitude. "Where were these explorers if not in the 'hollow earth?' and would they not have come out of the South Pole, if they had not changed their course?"

Clearly they had crossed the verge, and were sailing on the inner side, without knowing it, hence the dip of the needle, and the North Star over the stern of the ship.

"Admitting the earth to be a solid globe, and the cause of magnetism to be some attractive power at the pole, how could the needle vary differently on the same meridian

1051

in different latitudes, at the same period of time, or vary at the same place, at different periods of time? But admitting that the earth is a hollow sphere, it can be satisfactorily explained."

"The observations of modern astronomers have ascertained that the pole or axis of the earth is not always directed to the same fixed star, and of consequence that the axis does not always remain parallel to itself. This variation is discovered to be about fifty-one minutes annually, which would make a degree in about seventy-one years; hence the needle always pointing to the polar opening would vary in about that proportion at the same place in the same period of time."

"From an examination of the variation of the compass, as ascertained in different degrees of latitude and longitude, it increases as you proceed north and west, which would be exactly the case in accordance with the theory of concentric spheres."

Doctor Kane's U.S. explorations in 1853, 1854, and 1855, confirmed former expeditions as to a milder climate beyond the arctic circle, and we make the following quotations from his reports:

"June 20. No seals were seen the two preceding days, but today we saw several, and three dovekies. Latitude seventy-six, D.E. Mag., N. 32, degrees W. true."

"June 22. Birds, apparently ducks were seen in great numbers flying over the open waters, and while here we saw large flocks of geese.

"After passing three or four bluffs with small inlets, we got beyond the cliffs, where a new country opened on us. Here we saw nine seals in a small bay.

"About midnight I observed pieces of ice moving up the channel towards the north, at the rate of four knots per hour; and now when we are encamped, they are moving down the channel at the same rate.

"The ice here is entirely broken up, and the channel is navigable for vessels of any size. Eider ducks are so numerous that Hans killed two at one shot. Large flocks of geese are flying in shore and up the channel, and the rocks

1052

are covered with tern who are now breeding. Dovekies are very numerous, and ivory gulls and burgomasters have made their appearance.

"June 24. We saw a bear with a young one. Five of our dops gave chase. Hans shot the bear and killed her and the cub.

"Much grass was seen, as well as many plants. I climbed to the top of a knob over five hundred feet high, and from it there was not a speck of ice to be seen. As far as I could discern the sea was open, a swell coming in from the northward and running crosswise, as if with a small eastward set.

"Ivory gulls were nesting in rocks above me, and out to sea were molle-moke and silver-backed gulls.

"Petrels and gulls hung about the waves near the land.

"June 26. I cannot imagine what became of the ice. It must either go to an open space at the north or dissolve. The tides in shore seem to me both north and south, but the tide from the northward ran seven hours, and there was no slack water. The wind blew heavily down channel from the open water, and had been freshening since yesterday nearly to a gale, but brought no ice with it.

"June 28. The snow so soft that we sometimes sank to our knees in water. A great number of seals are seen." S.T. 50.

CAPTAIN HALL'S STATEMENTS.

Captain Hall steamed out of New York harbor in the Polaris, June 29, 1871. He pushed his way through ice up to the eighty-second degree and sixteen minutes, when he got into open water, and into a much warmer climate.

Newton says: "Above the eightieth degree of north latitude is one vast solitude of eternal ice up to the ninetieth degree," and this is the theory of geography and the so-called modern scientific teaching. But Captain Hall, and other explorers and navigators who have penetrated above eighty degrees, instead of eternal ice, find an open sea, warmer climate and abundant animal and vegetable life.

1053

THE HIDDEN WORLD

If Newton's theory of a solid globe is true, there would be eternal ice there. But melting snows, warm breezes, an open sea, the songs of birds, blooming flowers, and flowing currents, the variation of the needle, the North Star, all throw doubt upon his theory, and these circumstances, and proven facts, strongly point to the resistless conclusion of a hollow earth, and the chosen place where God has hidden the faithful Jews until He calls them to Jerusalem, when and where, a THIRD TEMPLE is to be erected, to endure forever.

Now Captain Buddington, who commanded the Polaris, was a believer in the Newtonian theory, and he refused to steam up to the eighty-third degree. Captain Hall could not prevail upon Captain Buddington to go any farther, and the captain went into winter quarters. The lookout reported that he could see forty miles to fifty miles northward, and there was no ice in the way. That all was open water, and he could also see a cloud up there that denoted water. Mr. Holby, Mr. Chester, Mr. Mier, and Captain Hall, all saw the open water and the cloud. Mr. Mier measured the distance and found it sixty-four miles to the cloud.

In spite of all persuasions to the contrary the vessel dropped back to eighty-one degrees and thirty-eight minutes, for winter quarters. S.T. 62.

Some days after Captain Hall and Mr. Chester went fifty miles north, on a sled, when they encountered an open sea, the waters of which were filled with shrimps, with numerous seals bobbing up their heads. Two of the seals were shot.

They could see land, and an open sea, for seventy miles, or up to eighty-three degrees and fifty-one minutes, and they saw a dark nimbus cloud in that direction that certainly indicated that beneath it was an open polar sea.

In his last dispatch to the Secretary of the U.S. Navy, Captain Hall said: "I find this a much warmer country than I expected, and it abounds with life, and seals, game, geese, ducks, musk cattle, deer, foxes, wolves, rabbits, partridges, lemmings with snipe, plover, and all kinds of wading birds."

This is official, and can be found on file at Washington, D.C., in the Navy Department. S.T. 62.

1054

Captain Hall died a few days afterwards, on the Polaris, with symptoms of having been poisoned by a cup of coffee. The expedition was abandoned at Hall's death and returned to the United States.

It is a great misfortune to science and the world, that Captain Hall died at this critical point, for now a cloud still hangs over the north, as dark as the "nimbus cloud" which he saw, and as he firmly believed it hung over the open polar sea.

How true it is, that man proposes but God disposes. Many brave and gallant men have dared the rigors of the polar climate, few ever reached the north part of the verge.

But Norwegians, English, Dutch, and Americans have attempted to solve the mystery, some have lived to return, others have perished on the way; and while Wiggins, Seebohm and the American whaler, Captain Tuttle, have heard Hebrew spoken, where science and Newton say is the region of eternal ice, we must admit that God has put His barriers up to hide the Lost Tribes of Israel. If they are there, hid in the earth, until He returns them to Jerusalem, the veil will remain down until the hand of the Almighty withdraws or lifts it himself. Among the latest efforts to cross the verge was that of Lieutenant Peary, who returned to St. John's, Newfoundland, September 15, 1894, and among other things, to illustrate the cold, reported, "that his dogs perished in great numbers and froze into solid chunks. On one occasion, he started with ninety-two dogs, and returned with but twenty-six, having lost sixty-six on the trip." No trace was found of the long-lost Swedish explorers, Bjorling and Raesteneus, who sailed in June, 1892, and have never been heard of since. Their death is now regarded as certain, or else they have crossed the verge, and are with the Children of Israel.

CHAPTER IX.

THE CLOUD MOVES.

THREE years after the events recorded in the last chapter, when Oratonga was present, a sudden loud,

1055

THE HIDDEN WORLD

prolonged and far-reaching blast of a trumpet was blown from the platform of the Altar of Burnt Offerings, which turned into sharp, short calls, and closed with a prolonged note which aroused every Hebrew in the encampment.

In answer to this, trumpets and horns rang out from the headquarters of all the tribes. A general and simultaneous movement was seen throughout the entire encampment. Tents commenced to come down, men, women and children were stirring around in a lively manner, packing for a march. Men selected from each tribe advanced and took down the outer inclosure around the tabernacle. Priest and Levites took off the three covers from the Tabernacle, rolled them up, put poles through the silver rings, took down the boards, enclosing the north and south sides, arranged the altars, brazen laver, and all things for marching. Horses, cattle, sheep, goats, etc., and fowls were brought in from the prairies, and all were ready for moving.

The cause of all this commotion and preparation was the action of the marvelous cloud. At the moment the first blast of the trumpet was heard the cloud, far up in the sky, had commenced gradually to lose its perpendicular, and began to bend towards the northwest, and slowly continued this movement, but at twelve the lower end over the place where the tabernacle lately stood majestically rose in the air, some two hundred feet, and steadily moved northwest.

At this moment all the Israelites were marking time to the beat of a drum, for a march, at their respective headquarters, and at the blast of a trumpet every foot came down, and the movement began at one moment and in military array. At the command "March," all started as one person. They moved in a hollow square. Armed men in front, rear, and on both flanks, the women and children in the front center, the animals behind them, with a squad of soldiers between the animals and women, so no accident or injury was likely to occur; they all slowly marched along, keeping step to the regular beat of drums. In the extreme front were the priests, carrying the Ark of the Covenant, and Melchisedec and Nardo walked at the head of the procession, and kept their eyes steadfastly upon the perpendicular and miraculous

1056

cloud, pursuing its silent course onward.

Whenever the people fell behind, for any cause, the cloud would tarry, remaining motionless until the Ark of the Covenant arrived under it, when it moved forward again. The usual distance was one mile an hour, and after traveling from four to six miles without halting, the cloud would stop, thereby signifying that the day's movement was over, and camp was immediately made. It always accommodated itself to them, stopping long enough for all their necessities.

The movement was leisurely done, and the cloud always stopped long enough for meals and the preparations for camping. And it had long been observed that they were never caught in rain or snow, nor in a storm of any kind. Although, it has not been heretofore mentioned, the march commenced in May, and ended in October, and during the rest of the year the cloud remained stationary, and so did the Israelites.

On the day we are now considering, the Hebrews had been years on the way, and they were at this time within the Arctic circle, and on the banks of a large river, flowing northwest, and how to cross it was the problem for the priests to solve.

The cloud rested, and the Israelites encamped. At this moment a man of venerable appearance, was seen standing on a high rock, on an island which rose in the river, and Melchisedec and Nardo went to the bank, when the stranger spoke and said to them:

"Tarry until the second day, and a crossing will be provided."

"All right," replied Melchisedec, and turning to Nardo he said:

"There will be another Jordan," and when he turned to look again for the stranger, lo, he had vanished. The lofty rock on which he stood and spoke was silent and deserted. A flock of wild geese were winging their way down the river, honking, as they went. A fish-hawk's harsh note was heard, as he few from the dry limb of a dead tree. A bald-headed eagle was passing just below the top of the rock where the strange man had been seen, and although they waited and looked for a long time and strained their eyes he was not

1057

THE HIDDEN WORLD

seen any more.

The swash of water, and the deep murmur of a broad and rapid river alone was heard, as its mighty current rushed headlong down the steep and winding channel.

Melchisedec and Nardo returned to the encampment, filled with wonder, and having thoughts which they did not communicate to each other.

AN EARTHQUAKE.

Before the dawn of day, a deep, hollow sound like the roar of thousands of cannons was heard, and the water of the river was tremendously agitated. The whole country trembled from the terrific shocks. The convulsion ceased for a short period, while the awful noise rolled and growled as it passed away.

Then it recommenced, as if deep down in the earth and from an immense distance away, but it advanced with great rapidity with roar after roar, and crash after crash, thundering on, with a terrific deafening noise. The water in the river was thrown high in the air, and, falling, was swallowed up by the earth in bottomless chasms. An indescribable, fearful noise was heard, apparently converging at the channel of the river, as if rocks were rent asunder, then followed a deep hollow murmur, and explosions of subterranean artillery was heard as if in retreat, like distant rumbling of thunder, far away; then the sounds ceased, the trembling stopped, and a silence so intense followed, that the frightened listeners could hear the throbbings of their own hearts.

While these dreadful happenings occurred, the pillar of fire, which always took the place of the cloud at night, spread out and around the Israelites, as if it were a wall of fiery protection. It so seemed, and it had all the time given them assurance that Jehovah was not forgetful of them during these awe-inspiring events.

The animals, the camp, and all it contained were illumined by this light. When the last sound of the subterranean thunder died out, and the trembling earth grew still, and the ground motionless, the light withdrew, and only the ordinary

1058

pillar of fire rose and pointed upwards towards the silent and fathomless sky. Reassured by the silence, and the evident providential protection, the Israelites retired to their tents, and the slow hours rolled on until the Sabbath came.

Melchisedec, was within the two thousand yards, the prescribed Sabbath day's journey, of the river, and he went to the bank, and a strange spectacle met his sight. The bed of the stream directly in front was dry, except here and there a little pool. A half a mile above him the water was pouring into the earth, raising a mist, and a beautiful rainbow arched across the middle of the falls. Where the river was flowing on Saturday night, so grandly and impetuously, now was a deep canon; ducks and geese were flying along below, squawking and honking, and winging their way down stream, evidently bewildered, and not comprehending the change in once familiar haunts.

The whirling waters rushed through a chasm hundreds of feet below him. But the strangest thing of all, and what seemed miraculous, was that a bridge of rocks composed of mica slate, half a mile wide and long reached across the chasm, from shore to shore, in front, and the lower end was attached to the perpendicular rock where the strange man had been seen.

The rocks at each end of this remarkable bridge appeared to be of a less tenacious substance, and had yielded more readily to the earthquake shock, and the disintegrating and grinding process of rock and water. Either the natural structure of the rock had made this natural bridge, or an overruling Providence had again manifested itself in favor of His chosen people. When Melchisedec remembered the stranger on the rock, he felt a thrill of joy, and he said devoutly to Nardo, while he pointed to the bridge:

"The hand of Jehovah! See, a bridge in front, deep chasms above and below!"

The two returned to camp and reported what they had seen. There was a general rejoicing and a general wonder and strengthening of faith among the people. On Monday the cloud gave the usual indications of a movement. As soon as the bending cloud indicated the course, a line of soldiers

THE HIDDEN WORLD

was placed along the bridge, at each side, and the children of Israel crossed between them and continued their journey.

It may strike some readers as singular that this strata of rocks was so much harder than the surrounding rocks, and that it should give them such a safe and secure footing; but it is not without a parallel in history of earthquakes, and I therefore cite the following from pages 501 and 502 of the Encyclopedia of Wonders and Curiosities, which reads as follows:

"The ground is frequently agitated with the most violent shocks. But sometimes, in the same rock, the superior strata form an invincible obstacle to the propagation of the motion. At Cumana, for instance, before the catastrophe of 1797, the earthquakes were felt only along the southern and calcareous coast of the Gulf of Cariaco, as far as the town of the same name, while in the peninsula of Araya and in the village of Marinaquez, the ground did not partake of the same agitation.

"The inhabitants of the northern coast, which is composed of mica slate, built their huts on a motionless earth; a gulf, three or four thousand fathoms in breadth, separated them from a plain covered with ruins and overturned by earthquakes."

But to return to the Tribes of Israel. After passing through ice fields, and the arctic regions, in which many manifestations of Divine protection were given, they moved on, day after day, and commenced to travel down over the verge, where it commences to descend into the earth.

As the reader has hitherto been advised, this was not a thing which the eye could observe, owing to the limited vision of man's sight. And the first thing to attract their attention, was what navigators have always noticed; it was the strange appearance of the visible horizon. They could see a long distance, right and left, but when they looked backwards or in front the sight was much shorter; and as they continued to move on one star after another disappeared from sight, and the moon appeared only for a short period of time, and then suddenly disappeared long before it should, as if it had dropped from the sky. It began to create

1060

THE HIDDEN WORLD

an idea that they were really going into a new land where they would indeed be hidden from the rest of the world. As they traveled only from May to November, they had crossed the arctic regions during the most favorable time and one of those favorable seasons related by the American whaler, Mr. Tuttle, mentioned in a former chapter. As they moved on day by day, the star field grew to be a narrowing belt, which became less and less as the crust of the earth shut out the field of the visible heavens.

But a few weeks since the migrating animals and birds on the outer crust of the earth were going south, and in an opposite direction to their course, but now they were going the same way with them, and this made some believe that Jehovah had done this to supply them with food. But now the climate was growing warmer and warmer with every week's movement, vegetable life and trees and grasses became larger and more plentiful, and the sun had never set for many days, but shone on and on, without any night, and the further they went the light of the sun grew gradually dimmer and dimmer. But a strange and beautful light was seen overhead that reached across the sky, as far as they could see, and this light gave out a steady and constant heat. After that, the glare of the sunshine, with a silvery radiance of a steady light, and finally no stars, or moon, or sun was seen, but overhead was this constant silvery light and heat.

As the vigilant reader has surmised, they had, without fully and completely understanding the matter, traveled down the verge and had gone into the hollow earth so far that the sun, moon, and stars were shut out, and they had electrical light, which illumines the inner world, as more fully explained hereafter.

Bible-readers will remember that there was a light spoken of before the sun was made, and that was electricity, which, as will presently appear, is in all bodies, and is everywhere present, wherever matter is to be found.

EXPLAINS NIGHT.

As the topography and climatic conditions are different

1061

THE HIDDEN WORLD

from the outer world, so are night and day.

Several agencies contribute to vary the movement of water, which produces the electric light for the inner world.

In revolving east and west, the earth carries the water in the oceans forward until they strike the shores of western continents, heaping them up there, making tides.

The moon as it sails over oceans attracts the water, which leaps up and follows its course, until, passing over the land, it releases its strong attraction, when the water flows back, thus making tides on the eastern shores.

A gulf stream plows its resistless course through the oceans. Thus the rotation of the earth, the moon, gulf stream, and trade winds keep the waters in ceaseless motion.

To these is added the heat of the sun on the exterior world.

This luminary in the daytime warms the oceans over the equator of each hemisphere; currents of heated water are created on the surface of the oceans, and flow along, while cold water from the inner world pours out at the verges, and at the submarine outlets in vast quantities, which at certain hours sensibly lessens the quantity of water in the inner world, pouring over the huge waterfalls therein, that lessens the friction, that reduces the quantity of electricity, for the electric sun, the light sensibly lessens with the receding water, thus producing a twilight, which is called night in the inner world, but at opposite time of the day from the outer world.

The nights are not so dark there as on the outer world, except about Hebron, as explained hereafter in another chapter, and around the cataracts of falling water, where those tremendous mists hang so dense forever.

The celebrated M. Dassie, on page 472, of The Encyclopedia of Wonders and Curiosities says:

"The sea has a general motion independent of wind and tides. This motion is from east to west, inclining towards the northern sign; but the contrary way, after the sun has passed said equinoctial southward, that when the general motion is changed, the diurnal flux changes also."

This diurnal motion of M. Dassie, along with winds,

1062

tides, moon, the rotation of the earth, the inrush and outflow at the verges and submarine outlets, the flux and reflux, resulting from all these agencies, produces the electricity in the manner explained for the inner world, and the phenomena of day and night.

It is only recently, in this century, so prolific and daring in thought and mighty discoveries, that it is claimed that we are living ourselves in a hollow world.

That the sun is the center of a circle, that the stars and moon and planets constituting our solar system are all revolving around the sun, and all are surrounded by a casing in which all are spinning in a circle called creation, outside of which is utter, vast, profound darkness.

Science has demonstrated the fact that our earth is lighter than some other worlds, and when convinced that our earth may be a hollow sphere, we can then regard it in God's hands, like a soap-bubble in the air.

It is now known that ether has in it aragon, apparently lighter than air, which is found to be the most powerful, most subtle element filling all space, and is the all-prevailing power which holds all things solid throughout the universe, and communicates intelligent thoughts to the absent and beloved.

But these things, while food for the inquisitive and philosophical, do not concern us, as this book is limited in its scope, to disclose the whereabouts of the lost races of Israel, so often referred to in the Bible.

CHAPTER X.

THE AURORA BOREALIS.

ONE of the peculiarities noticed by the Israelites in their journey was the appearance of the Aurora Borealis, north and south of the verge. The streams of light south of the verge seemed to rise immediately from the ground, and stream off as if radiating from some central point, and then spreading out like the light from the sun.

"The luminous rays of light were generally of a reddish

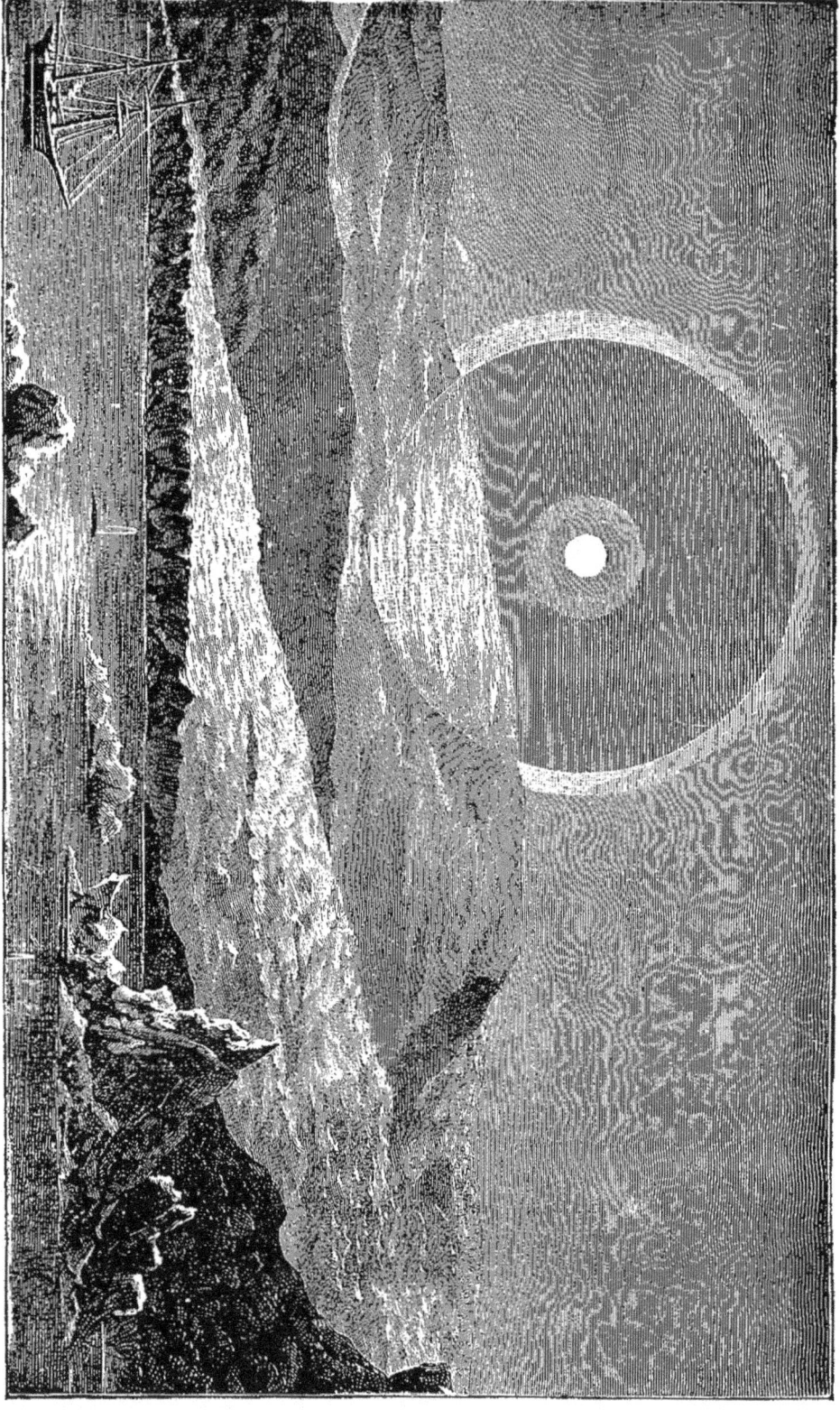
AURORA BOREALIS ON THE OUTER WORLD.

THE HIDDEN WORLD

color, fading into yellow, and flashing out coruscations of pale light, darting from the low horizon with great velocity up to the zenith. Sometimes they remained motionless, then with marvelous rapidity they streamed out into thousands of sparkling rays, with all the known colors, from the most vivid down to an obscure russet; they assumed the shape of columns, then slowly changed to ten thousand varied shapes. They occasionally covered all the northern hemisphere, and then they astonished and awed the beholder. Then they paled away, and suddenly burst out and flashed in brilliant illuminations, and darted away into the heavens, have tremlous spasms, and then fade away so imperceptibly that the spectator looks upon the sky and cannot tell the exact time of their evanishment. Few can behold these marvelous lights without a mingled feeling of awe and terror. These displays are sometimes noiseless, and sometimes with a hissing sound rushing through the air, as if fireworks were at play." "The hunters who pursue the white and blue foxes in the confines of the icy sea, are often alarmed in their course by these northern lights. The dogs are then so much frightened that they will not move, but lie obstinately on the ground till the noise has passed." - C.W.E.W.C., pp. 684-688. "Messrs. Gmelin, Nairne, Belknap, and Cavalls also speak of these hissing noises."

It is important also to state that Captain Cook saw similar phenomena and lights playing around what is called the South Pole, all of which confirms the idea of a hollow world inside of this globe.

The extraordinary appearance of the Aurora Borealis was seen and described by Captain Parry in his expedition to the arctic regions: "Seen at different places and at different latitudes, Aurora Borealis presents many singular phases, and are incomprehensible to man. Dr. Blagden has seen them join and form luminous balls, darting about with great velocity, and even leaving a train behind them like common fireballs."

Whether these remarkable electrical and unexplainable appearances dart like streams of electricity from the north and south extremities of our globe, and meet with returning

1065

AURORA BOREALIS, SEEN FROM THE INNER WORLD.

electricity beyond the limits of earth's atmosphere, shoot out from the sun, and clash and dance at a great distance in the sky, to mystify and amaze mankind, they are among the hidden mysteries, proclaiming the unspeakable majesty and glory of God. On His almighty throne as He looks upon the earth, spinning in space, and obeying the laws He has ordained, He sees lights shining at the North and South poles, they being the Aurora Borealis to us. While man has lived upon the earth thousands and thousands of years, without knowing the secrets of God hidden at the north and south. He has sailed around the earth, east and west, but north and south are as mysterious to him as the source of the Nile was once to geography, and as unknown as electricity is today. That part of the world at 90 degrees is today terra incognita.

While science and conjecture are at fault, we hope further on to give some reasonable explanations of those marvels upon well-known physical and dynamic laws, which may not be considered satisfactory, but which cultured and fair-minded readers will concede to be reasonable, to some extent, and which will not conflict with matter and laws supposed to be well established. Captain Cook, speaking of these strange southern lights, says:

"On February 17, 1773, in South latitude 58 degrees a beautiful phenomenon was observed during the preceding nights. It consisted of long columns of clear white light, shooting up from the horizon to the eastward, almost to the zenith, and gradually spreading on the whole southern part of the sky. The columns were sometimes bent sidewise at their upper extremities, and though in most respects similar to the northern lights of our hemisphere, yet they differed from them in being always of a white color, whereas ours assume various tints, especially of fiery purple color." - C.W.E.W.C., pp. 686 and 687.

Father Boscovish, determined the height of an aurora observed on the 16th of December, 1737, by the Marquis of of Poleni, to have been eight hundred and twenty-five miles; and Mr. Bergman, from a mean of thirty computations, makes the average height of the Aurora Borealis, four hundred and sixty Eng. miles. Mr. Euler supposes the height to be several thousand miles, and Mr. Blagden says: "The great accumulation of electrical matter seems to lie beyond the verge of our atmosphere, as estimated by the cessation of twilight." - G.W.E.W.C., p. 683. If the Borealis goes beyond twilight and extends into the boundaries of eternal night, it is indeed a wonderful and obscure secret of nature.

But leaving the field of conjecture after we have presented to the reader the appearance of the Aurora Borealis, as seen by the Israelites, after passing the verge, and still looking backwards towards the north, the on-moving cloud led them south, and the North Star was left behind them, when, as they understood the compass, they were all the time supposing that they were going north. It presented to them the enigma of a man all the while traveling east, in going around the world, and traveling east he will come back to the point he started from and from the west. And so a man starting around the world north, and always traveling north, he would appear to travel north, but would come back to the point of starting and still be faced to the north.

CHAPTER XI.

CHANGED TOPOGRAPHY.

WHAT struck the Israelites most forcibly on crossing the verge, was the radical difference in the distribution of the land and water. Ever since the high-priest, by his drawings, had disclosed a hollow earth, and its interior as their destination, they had followed the cloud by day, and the pillar of fire by night, with perfect faith and without murmuring, and reasonably prepared to accept all strange events and marvelous displays of God's power, for they had long since learned that all things were possible to Him.

The displays of providential protection on the prairies, among the mountains, icebergs, and the manna for the Sabbath day, met the requirements of the most exacting, but to find rivers, islands, mountains, and continents, where hills, lakes, valleys, and oceans were, on the outer world,

THE HIDDEN WORLD

was a wonderful and unexpected surprise; and their continual advance and final explorations taught them to look everywhere for a direct variation in the topography and geography of the country, and a consequent different distribution of the animal, vegetable, and climatic conditions. Where Davis' Strait, and Baffin's Bay, Behring Strait, and the Gulf of Obi, were, on the maps of earth, were mountains and isthmuses leading to continental elevations.

North America, South America, Europe, Asia, Africa, Australia, were oceans, and the East and West Indies were lakes. Where our loftiest mountains appeared were deep valleys, hills, gently rolling bluffs, or broad extended plains, pampas, or prairies. The beds of the Mississippi, Amazon, Nile, Danube, Indus, Kinsha-Kiang, the Ho-Hango, and large rivers on the surface of the exterior world, were the tops of mountain ranges, corresponding to the Rocky Mountains, the Andes, the Ural, and Himalaya mountains of earth. And they soon discovered, to their satisfaction, some of the prominent causes for the currents in the oceans, the source of springs and rivers, and the tides on the outer world where we live. The abrupt and sudden flow from the oceans on the outside to the oceans within cause currents to sweep through the exterior, and interior oceans, the greater attraction of the interior, caused by shrinking of surface from twenty-five thousand miles, on the exterior, to twelve thousand within, concentrated the gravity therein, making it stronger there, and moved the waters with accelerated speed; and the large surface exposed on the exterior warmed the water on the equatorial regions, and the everlasting flow of the water, to obtain an equilibrium, kept them in constant motion, and the attraction of the moon on the surface of the earth, and it having no attraction within, but sailing around the exterior world, all contributed to keep the water in everlasting motion. Also the deep waters within the valleys, underlying the mountains, supplied them with exhaustless volumes of water, ever coming and going, and thus springs, fountains, and streams gushed out among hills, and mountains, and each part of the earth's crust by reciprocal interchange of diverse topographical arrangement within and without, mani-

1069

fested the wisdom of the divine Architect who planned and directed the same when the earth was created. And man has been made intelligent enough to understand wherever he sees them that they are the footprints of the Creator.

To make our idea clearer, it is to be remembered that beneath the Rocky Mountains, on the under world, is a deep sea, and the deepest part is under the Rocky Mountains, and the immense pressure of the water fills all the interstices in the rock, all cracks, where the upheaval rent them, and the water percolating through the rock and soil dissolves the salt which is deposited, and when the water leaps out to the upper crust of the earth it becomes fresh, and it finds its way in fountains, springs, brooks, creeks, and they, pouring into a common channel, form lakes and rivers, which flow back to the ocean; and this, with the mist blown inland, and condensed on the mountains and cold stratas of air, fall in rain and snow; and these with the agencies of heat, and cold, keep the earth constantly supplied with water for animals and the vegetable world, and for man, inside and outside, according to laws God provided at the beginning; thus all parts of the globe, inside and outside, are cared for by fixed and immutable laws.

CHAPTER XII.

NARDO'S HUNTING ADVENTURE.

WHILE they were encamped, on one occasion, Nardo concluded to go hunting, and on the way he called to see Rebecca, and while there a flock of wild geese lighted in a large pond not far away, and, observing them, he said:

"Excuse me for a short time, while I try my luck with these geese." And being excused he departed; but as he left, Rebecca said:

"Be careful, the swamp is treacherous and bottomless!"

"Never fear for me," said Nardo, as he waved his hand in adieu.

He then disappeared, and going behind bushes, he carefully approached, and when within good bow shot, he took careful aim, drew the string taut, and let his arrow go. It proved to be a center shot, and a noble goose flopped his wings, turned on his back, while the others arose in wild confusion, gathered in a flock, and flew away with loud honking.

When Rebecca saw them on the wing, she went out to the pond to discover what her lover's success was. She discovered Nardo placing limbs, poles and brush upon the thick grass which grew between the shore and the clear water, making a rude bridge to support him, so he could get his game.

With the instinct of true wisdom which is one of nature's gifts to woman, she feared for her lover, and without speaking to him she hastened back to her tent, and taking a roll of ropes which all tenting people keep on hand, she started for Nardo, and as she left her tent she said to her maid:

"Rachel, take a roll of ropes, follow me, tie one end of the rope to a stout tree and throw the other to me, if I motion to you. Hurry!"

After this rapid order, Rebecca, with quick footsteps, hastened towards her lover. She soon discovered him, standing on a collection of sticks and limbs, holding in his hands the body of a small sapling, about four inches in diameter, which he sought to throw across a spot of clear water upon a muskrat house, to cross upon it and reach the dead goose, whose right wing had lodged on the other side of the house. The muskrat house rose about eighteen inches above the water, and it looked strong enough to hold up a man, provided the foundation reached down to a solid bottom.

Rebecca took in the situation at a glance. With a silent motion she beckoned to Rachel to advance and tie one end of the rope to a tree and the other she tied around her body, and also to the rope she carried in her hands. While this was being done she glanced over the way between herself and her lover, and saw that thick coarse grass and flags had grown up through the ooze and mud and water, to the spot where Nardo stood, and if a person stepped lightly and quickly all would be well, but if one stopped for ever so short a time the water would rise around his feet, and then

1071

break through, and that would be the last of him, for the ooze and treacherous mud and quicksand would engulf all living things.

While considering this danger, not far away she saw a place where a hunter and his dog had been swallowed up but a week before, and the dark place in the grass where the water showed made her shudder as she beheld it.

Here and there she saw with dismay the water appearing, where the line of brush and limbs had been placed by Nardo as he went out to the clear water near the muskrat house.

Pointing to the water spots she whispered to Rachel:

"Brush and sticks, quick!"

The black eyes of the maid shone with added fire as she nodded and started to comply.

Meanwhile, Nardo had thrown his pole on to the muskrat house, and with active and careful steps, crossed, and had reached the goose, and catching the wing, drew up his game and gazed a moment at it. The weight of the bird, man, and pole was too much, and the rat house began slowly to sink. Quickly comprehending his danger, Nardo turned and flung the goose towards and on to the grass. It landed safely, but the jar under his feet caused the muskrat house to sink more rapidly, and when Nardo attempted to go back, it left his feet suddenly, and he found himself in the water, and down he went out of sight.

But he was a good swimmer, and up he came, and two or three strokes carried him to the grass, but when he grasped it, it gave away, and then he realized for the first time his great peril. In grasping the grass his hand touched the pole; he clutched it and tried to touch the bottom, but it went down and down to the end, and he just felt a perceptible touch when it struck the ooze and sunk without resistance, and then he knew how desperate his case was. Lamenting his foolishness in going after the game, he struck for the grass and brush, but as soon as he attempted to lift himself up it all gave way, and down he went under the water; he became tangled up in the grass and brush, and when he rose to the surface, as he did by a powerful effort, he found the tangled grass twining around his legs. His strength was giving away,

1072

and he feared his time had come. He put one hand down to pull the grass from his feet, and went under the water like a shot. With a desperate effort he arose to the surface, and caught sight of Rebecca, and as a rope flashed by him she said:

"Catch the rope, dear, catch it!"

Quick as a flash he grasped the rope, and by its aid arose above the water, and caught sight of the pale and troubled countenance of his sweetheart. The extra strain caused the feet of Rebecca to sink, and she cried out:

"Tie the rope to your body, I am sinking."

Without an instant's hesitation Nardo looped the rope around his body, and tied it fast, and as he did so, with a scream Rebecca commenced going down through the grass, which gave way under her feet. A strong pull upon the rope kept her head above the water. The space between her and Nardo was only a few feet, and brush and sticks lay on the grass, which had hitherto withstood the heavy pull, but Nardo saw with dismay that they were slowly sinking and bubbles of air were beginning to rise. The creaking of the grass and brush told the strain, and Nardo knew a catastrophe was near at hand.

Rebecca turned her head towards the shore, and said, "Run, Rachel, run, and scream for help!"

The Jewish maiden, brought to her senses, screamed with mortal terror, running with all her might, for camp, and uttering scream after scream. Presently she was stopped by a hunter, who said,

"In the name of Moses and Aaron what's the matter?"

Rachel turned and ran back towards the fatal pond, crying as she went:

"Come! come! for the Lord's sake! they are drowning! Oh, the Lord help them!"

Knowing something dreadful had happened, the Jew pursued the fleeing Rachel, but as he ran he drew a whistle and blew rapid and shrill notes of alarm which were heard for a long distance. During the absence of Rachel, the following events had happened to our lovers, and Nardo said:

"Rebecca, pull steady on the rope toward the shore,

1073

I'll pull enough to keep our heads above the water, until help comes." But even as he spoke, the treacherous grass gave away, and down went the brush, grass, Nardo, and Rebecca all out of sight. Clutching the rope Nardo pulled himself to Rebecca, put his left arm around her waist, pulled desperately on the rope towards the shore, and raised both their heads above the water. Fortunately the rope lay across a larger limb which held them quite firmly. But when Rebecca arose she was strangled; she threw her arms around wildly, coughing and strangling all the while. Nardo put her chin across the rope and said:

"Rebecca, you are safe." She heard his voice, looked wildly, and throwing her arms around him they both went under the water like a rock. Nardo struggled hard to come to the surface, but his hold had been torn from the rope, and folding both arms around Rebecca, when he went under the water for the last time, he sent up a silent prayer to God, and became insensible. Meantime Jew and Jewess arrived at the tree, and grasping the rope tugged with all their might, and brought the lovers to the top of the water. But the strain on the rope cut the grass, and they sank as often as they were pulled to the surface. Meantime the shrill whistles brought a dozen men, and grasping the rope, by main force, a mass of grass, brush, and Nardo and Rebecca were drawn to the shore. The lovers were tightly clasped in each other's arms, and Rebecca's long hair was wrapped around the neck of Nardo. A sharp knife severed her beautiful hair, and the lovers were laid out on the ground apparently dead.

By direction of an aged Hebrew they were turned face downwards, their bodies lifted a little, and the water ran out of their mouths. Their arms were lifted and worked in such a manner as to force the water out of their lungs. Air was blown strongly into their nostrils, the mouth firmly closed, and the chest of each was raised and contracted by working the arms up and down, thus imitating breathing, and, after a time, the heart of each one beat faintly a few times, and then ceased. But constant and continued exertion finally triumphed, and, while insensible, they were put upon im-

1074

provised stretchers and borne carefully to Rebecca's tent. The beating of pulse and heart gave hope that the lovers, although insensible, might ultimately recover, and here we leave them for the present in the hands of their friends.

CHAPTER XIII.

ENCHANTING COUNTRY. FIGHT WITH PECCARIES.

THEIR journeying brought the Israelites to a country full of game, apples, plums, grapes and peaches.

They were now traveling along a stream that grew larger as they progressed, into which numerous small streams flowed, with fertile valleys and beautiful rolling hills. Deer, wolves, rabbits, prairie-chickens, quails, turkeys, and songbirds were abundant.

The river-bottoms were about equally divided into prairie and woodlands. The stream wound across the valley, and along its banks, oak, ash, walnut, hickory and sycamore grew.

At nearly every bend of the river, between it and the low-rolling bluffs, were extensive thickets of wild plums, overgrown with grapes, and along the borders were hazel thickets, in which rabbits took shelter, and often deer, disturbed, would bound up and go loping along, their ears erect, nostrils distended, and their white tails in the air. Occasionally flocks of wild turkeys would be seen, but by running and flying they would soon disappear. The animals generally were not very wild, having never before seen man. They merely moved out of the way, and gazed in dumb and bewildering amazement upon them. It was soon noticed that the sound of trumpet and drum frightened them amazingly, and they all took to flight or wing as soon as either was heard.

As they progressed the bluffs grew into hills, keeping pace by some law in height to the width of the river. After these hills had assumed higher altitudes at the foot, and for some distance up, they observed patches of blackberry bushes, so thick and tangled that it was difficult in some places to get through. But what filled them with the greatest surprise was that up beyond the blackberries, the side and summit, and, as they afterwards learned, for miles back, the entire land was covered with apple trees. The vastness and extent surpassed all belief. These orchards extended sometimes sixty miles along their way, and often forty miles wide, back over the rolling hills. This was a novel sight indeed, and never seen on the outer world, except on the Sandwich Islands, where there is an orchard on the side of a mountain sixty miles long, and forty deep. But these vast orchards astonished the Hebrews, and apples by countless bushels lay on the sidehills, and were piled up many feet deep in the hollows and ravines, while the trees were many of them loaded down with fruit in different stages of ripening.

The whole air was full of the odor of apples, as soon as one approached near these extensive orchards.

Scores of bears, wild hogs, and deer, were feeding on the fallen fruit, separated into groups, and giving no more attention to each other than having sentinels on the lookout for danger; when the bears or wild hogs shifted from place to place the deer would move on, apparently giving way to their more robust and aggressive neighbors.

The cloud tarried on one occasion near one of these orchards, and after encamping, a party was sent out to gather apples, an order which was gladly obeyed.

On the approach of the apple-gatherers the deer moved readily away. The wild hogs lifted their heads, sniffed the air, and seemed disinclined to move. An old patriarch, and evidently a leader, advanced a few paces, champed his jaws, and showed his long tusks, shaking his head savagely, while the pigs and younger hogs gathered in a bunch and gazed on the soldiers and their leader and protector. Several other large hogs came forward and formed a line abreast, but a little distance back of a straight line with the leader. Seeing the firm and hostile appearance of the wild hogs, the men in advance of the apple-gatherers halted, and a line of men and hogs confronted each other.

At this moment a squad of men came from the camp, and

1076

with them a lot of dogs. The moment the dogs saw the hogs, they set up yelping, and, encouraged by the men, they charged headlong in a body, and a terrible hubbub ensued. The hogs stood their ground, threw some of the dogs up, ran down others; while the hogs standing at bay rushed in, and all the dogs were soon killed or beat a hasty retreat. Some of the fleeing dogs ran towards the men, others, with tails between their legs, struck a bee-line for camp. When the dogs were routed, they were pursued by the hogs, who, when they saw the men, halted, shook their heads, advanced a few steps, stamped their feet, champed their jaws, their eyes shining with fury. The line of hogs grew larger each moment, and more threatening. There were but about fifty men, and without arms, for they had been left behind, and the men thought best to slowly give way; but at the first backward step to the rear, the hogs charged in a body, and all the men could do was to mount the nearest apple trees, and soon the chosen people of the Lord were, like Zaccheus, up a tree.

The animals charged around, ripped the bark with their tusks, stood on their hind feet, with the front ones against the trees, and tried in vain to reach the treed Israelites. It happened that some boys who had followed the men, and had been gathering apples that rolled down beyond the blackberry bushes, saw the treed men, and ran to camp and gave an alarm.

A body of five hundred spearmen and bowmen started out with drums beating and trumpets sounding to their rescue.

It was a welcome sound to the treed men, and when they caught sight of the gleaming spears, they shouted aloud and were greatly relieved. The hogs grew still, looked up at the men, lowered their heads, and listened to the roll of the advancing drums, and the prolonged blasts of the trumpets. It was the first time that martial music ever pealed through these Arcadian isles, and it seemed to have a terrifying effect upon a majority of the hogs. Their bristles and waving tails came down, and now here, and now there, a hog moved away, at first in a slow walk, then into a trot, and finally

THE HIDDEN WORLD

into a precipitate run.

A few of the older ones stood their ground, especially those whose blood had been up fighting the dogs. The men in the trees shouted, and laughed aloud; the advancing soldiers with drums beating and leveled spears burst through the blackberry bushes with loud shouts and away went the last of the hogs on a dead run, amid the jeers of the soldiers, who only caught a sight of vanishing tails. The soldiers were ordered to "stack arms, disperse, and regale themselves on apples," except a guard to protect the arms. This first was an order eagerly obeyed, and soon the soldiers were scattered around, gathering the tempting fruit. While roaming through the vast orchard, tasting and selecting the best fruit, some of them crossed a little ravine, and ascended the opposite hill, lured on by some specially attractive red apples. On the way a young captain made fun of a companion who had been treed by the hogs, and, on arriving at the brow of the hill, and halfway down the hither slope, they saw a conflict between a large bear and a group of peccaries. The bear was so covered up and surrounded that it was a little time before they could tell what it was. But the bear succeeded in throwing off his assailants for a second, and bloody, discomfited, and defeated, the bear tried to escape, and it happened that he came directly towards them. The peccaries, furious with rage, ran behind, at his side, in front, jumping on and cruelly cutting him with their sharp teeth. The man who had been treed by the wild hogs immediately turned and fled, but the young captain drew his short sword, and holding it in his left hand, threw a large apple and waved his arms, trying to intimidate them.

It was a grave mistake when the young captain threw and tried to "scare" away the peccaries, for the bear was soon overtaken, borne to the ground, cut all over, and, bleeding at every wound, fell limp and helpless, covered over by peccaries, who now tore him round and round and rent him in pieces, and soon there was no semblance of a bear.

A few peccaries, attracted to the captain, plunged head-

1078

long at him. He was as brave as rash, and received them as best he could, but they jumped so swiftly, cut at his legs, and were so active and ferocious that he could not maintain the fight. He succeeded in cutting two or three legs, so they fell, cut off several ears, wounded some in the head, cut some on the nose, put out some eyes, but the wounded never relaxed their efforts, and he saw them coming in all directions, and turning, he ran with all speed under an apple tree whose branches were within his reach by jumping; he leaped up, drew up his limbs, and, being an athlete, he swung up his feet and was just above the reach of the jumping peccaries. They would draw back a short distance, run swiftly, and jump up at him, snapping as they went by; to place himself out of danger, he climbed to a higher limb, but he was bleeding from numerous wounds, his clothes were torn, and he felt faint and sick. Below him the ground was covered with peccaries, their fierce eyes uplifted. They champed, shook their heads, and gave shrill savage calls. A squad of them were tearing the bear to pieces, and slashing his bones around, as if wreaking vengeance upon their fallen foe. At this moment he heard the drum beat, the trumpet sound, and he caught the glimpse of spears as they flashed here and there among the trees. But while this cheered him, he was amazed at the wonderful number of peccaries. They came in a run from all quarters. The tumult of the fleeing wild hogs, the fight with the bear, the loud tumult about the treed man, seemed to have extended for miles around, and when the soldiers drew near hundreds of infuriated peccaries were snapping their jaws in rage and leaping at the treed man. When the soldiers drew near the captain cried out, "Here I am, treed, desperately wounded, and safe for the present, if I don't bleed to death. How many soldiers are you?"

"About one hundred."

"Stop where you are, form a hollow square ten or fifteen feet deep, the front ranks kneel, prepare to repel cavalry, have solid ranks of spears - or you will be overcome - there are thousands of these vicious animals in sight, and more coming."

1079

"A man in a tree is always a coward, we'll soon scatter these little pigs," replied the commander.

"Tolemeo, we were friends in Judea, for the sake of Abraham, Isaac, and Jacob, hear me. Send back to Alexo Strado, our commander, the warning I have given, tell him to form the men as I have requested, in open ground. He will heed my request. Do this before you advance further."

"For the sake of old Judea, and for the honored name of Abraham, Isaac, and Jacob, Johan Dorito, I'll do that, and then I'll see that you are court-martialed for cowardice – a soldier treed by pigs! Ha!"

A message was sent to Alexo Strado, and then the order to march was given, and a line of spears glittered as the soldiers advanced in three columns, with leveled spears at a charge. The peccaries had been acting queerly during this conversation, which had been conducted in a high key; they looked up towards Johna Dorito, while he was calling, and they turned their heads as the voice of Tolemeo came rolling over the swell. By animal instinct they comprehended that their foe was saying something to their enemy, but they could see Dorito, and that held them with implacable hatred to watch and guard him.

But when the line of soldiers came in sight there was no more hesitation, and, as moved by one common impulse, they charged headlong upon the soldiers. Scarcely had the command to "lower spears" been given before the peccaries were upon them. The three lines of spears impaled a hundred of them.

Before their bodies could be shaken off, others rushed and leaped over, and others came on the side, and attacked them in flank and rear, and soon a wild mass of struggling men and peccaries were engaged in a terrible conflict. The line of soldiers lost its military order in a short time. Peccaries by the dozen attacked each man, jumping and snapping in front, rear, cutting with their sharp tusks, ripping up their legs, and in a few minutes there was not an unwounded man.

Tolemeo was soon forced back, and fought valiantly. In the desperate struggle his sword pierced a large peccary, which leaped at his throat, and as the beast fell, his sword, which went deep in the beast, could not be withdrawn, and it was wrenched from his hand, and he was weaponless. He attempted to climb into the same tree with Johan Dorito, and he would have failed and been killed, but Dorito extended a helping hand, and he was soon beside the man who was to be "court-martialed for cowardice, in being treed by pigs. Ha!"

Tolemeo, seeing his soldiers would be destroyed, lifted his trumpet and sounded a retreat; and then crying out said, "All who can, retreat to the command; the wounded climb trees!"

It needed no second command, and those who were able to run did so, and with all their might, while others dropped their spears, and climbed up the trees. The largest number broke for camp, with the peccaries in hot pursuit.

Tolemeo sounded a continuous retreat, and it advised Alexo Strado, of the desperate state of affairs. In the meantime, when he received the message sent by Dorito, he had marched his men into the open prairie, and placed them in front of a ledge of rocks, which rose some thirty feet perpendicular, for about one hundred and fifty feet in length, and then tapered down at each end or flank, so men could scramble up. On the top of this rock he stationed his bowmen, and his spearmen he formed below in a half moon, each flank resting on the precipitous rocks which rose straight above them; some men lay flat on the ground, spears to the front, others kneeled between them, others bent down, and others formed standing, so that solid wall of spears rose from the ground six feet high, presenting a line of twenty spears deep, an impregnable and solid wall of defense.

The butts of many spears rested on the ground. Meantime the retreat, sounded by Tolemeo, had been heard at camp. The prolonged and continuous sound indicated great peril, and a demand for immediate relief. In a short time three thousand men started to his aid. And now just as Alexo Strado had completed his arrangement for defence, the fleeing men poured out of the bushes, pursued by hundreds of peccaries, leaping and fighting the fleeing Israelites. It was a wild and exciting chase - comical, dangerous, and

1081

savage. Most of the men had thrown away their spears, but retained their short swords, and as they fled they cut and slashed when they could, and many peccaries lost limbs, and such fell behind; but for every disabled one twenty more took its place. On came the tumultuous throng in wild savage array. When the flying men neared their comrades, they saw the line of spears, and turned abruptly, right and left, while the mass of peccaries plunged headlong upon the spears. Over three hundred were transfixed at the first onset, others sprung on the slain, and soon a wall of slaughtered peccaries attested the solidity of the line of spears. The ranks remained unbroken. The dead were shaken off as soon as possible, while other infuriated beasts took their place, only to meet the same fate.

Peccaries are like knights of Orient, they never retreat. They die or are victorious. All who know anything about them, will testify that they know no fear, never retreat, never yield; and the only way is to kill them or climb beyond their reach.

The bowmen on the rocks kept a constant discharge of arrows, and piles of dead and wounded peccaries were struggling and fighting about the line of spears. Though present in thousands they could not break the solid lines of Alexo Strado.

This slaughter continued for half an hour, when three thousand men came up. The drums beat, the trumpets sounded, and the contest continued until all the peccaries were slain; and no battle was ever more cumbered with the dead, or bloodier, or more sanguinary, than the one known as the battle of the bloody orchard with the peccaries. It should have been called "The Treed Israelites." Tolemeo and Johan Dorito were brought in on stretchers. But Tolemeo never demanded a court-martial for "being treed by pigs;" and thus ended the battle with the sanguinary peccaries.

CHAPTER XIV.

SOUTHWARD MOVEMENT - HAPPY ISLE.

AFTER the fight with the peccaries, the Israelites moved southward. The river grew large and deep; the land

THE HIDDEN WORLD

spread out into broad prairies, intersected by gently-flowing streams, and they traversed a country four hundred miles long and three hundred wide, and of surpassing beauty and fertility. The soil was a rich, black alluvial, mixed with sand, and was covered with abundant grass and countless flowers. Along the streams were forests, and the remainder was composed of level and rolling prairies, exceedingly rich and beautiful. Immense herds of buffaloes and deer were seen browsing. One of the impressive scenes was the countless flocks of prairie-chickens. Morning and evening flocks miles long and deep flew overhead, darkening the sky, and the noise of their wings was like a great wind. They finally came to where this mighty river emptied into the great ocean which underlies the North and South American continents. And here a most remarkable spectacle burst upon their view. Mountains of rock rose perpendicular before them at the right and left to a prodigious height, making further progress impossible. The waters in all directions, except in front, poured down into a chasm a mile deep all along the continental trend of the North and South American continents, as marked on the exterior maps of the world. The noise of falling waters was so vast, deep, and so tremendous, that all stood appalled. Clouds of mist rose over the abyss like vapor, and the friction was so prodigious that streams of electricity rose far above the clouds and streamed miles above them, forming a continuous line, running north and south in great waves of luminous light. The cloud rested here for a long time. Exploring parties were sent out east and west, and new and strange wonders discovered. The line of rocks reached far east and west, and when they had crossed, in the under world, that part of the exterior earth which we call the Atlantic Continent, to the European and African shores, the oceans were there found pouring their waters into a gulf as deep and more awful than on the American side. Everywhere the line of rocks cut off any approach to the inner oceans, except for a space of about five hundred miles wide, in a straight longitudinal line from north to south, which the geographers of earth would call the axis of the earth, or, rather, of the north and south poles. Far up overhead was a line of elec-

1083

trical light reaching to the ends of the earth and streaming out into open space, and making the pale light which scientists have observed, and which constitute the twilight and the aurora borealis. The tremendous concussions of all the oceans underneath the North and South American continents, and the continents of Europe, Asia, and Africa pouring into this profound abyss created an incomputable amount of electricity, which, rising upwards, joined the current of electricity from the north and south ends of the earth.

Far out in the midst of these clashing waters, and out so far that the waters became placid, and island of wonderful beauty, transcending all that mortal eyes had ever seen, reposed in serene and tranquil loveliness.

The tremendous noises and commotions of these falling oceans never disturbed its tranquil shores, and for two hundred miles around it the waters were always smooth and never disturbed by storms, and were of a bright silvery hue. The falling waters of all the world into this profound abyss created the incomputable mass of electricity already referred to, which, rising on high, collected in a great globe, or sun of electricity, above the island, and gave light and heat sufficient to make this center of earth the most delightful climate ever known or dreamed about. This electric sun was two thousand miles high in the exact center of the open sphere, three hundred miles in diameter, nine hundred miles in circumference, and shafts of electric light a hundred miles in diameter, and three hundred in circumference, streamed out at each pole, and meeting the electrical currents from the sun, held the world spinning in space and causing the twilight of the poles, and the aurora borealis, so strange and mysterious to man. It is known to scientists that the positive and negative electricity repel and attract each other. Two north poles of a magnet repel each other. So in a like manner do two south poles; but a north and south magnet attract and cohere together.

This wonderful arrangement of attraction and repulsion holds the earth from flying off into space or dropping into the sun. An electric rope through the open ends of the earth keeps the globe in place, enlivens the water, electrifies the

1084

THE HIDDEN WORLD

air, and holds all where the law of God placed them at creation.

Man uses electricity for lighting and power and understands it not. But He who dwells in heaven and whose footstool is the earth comprehends it all. There was but one spot to enter this charming scene, at the open place towards the north end of the world. The towering rocks, and the ocean plunging into the profound abyss were everlasting barriers elsewhere. The mist was so dense, that none but a dim light could penetrate the open space at the spot where the foaming waters plunged into the chasm and rolled for miles out; and so a line of semi-darkness hung over and around the falls, and a profound noise could be heard in those Stygian regions. But outside the lofty ridge of rocks, and over the lovely island, and through all the other skies the reflected and refracted sunshine of earth and the electric sun gave out their mingling rays, making a softer and more delightful light, than the blistering beams of the sun, on the outer side of the world, which blackens and darkens the skin of man in the torrid, and whitens it in the temperate zones.

Storms often beat in at the open spaces along the decline of the verge at the north and south ends of the earth. They come roaring down the verges. But they stop when the currents of auroral light stream out and meet them, for the electrical power is an immediate corrector of aerial disturbances. An equilibrium is thus restored, and storms of rain or snow never disturb the inhabitants 30 degrees within the verges. The mists from the prodigious waterfalls descend upon the mountain-tops of the inner world and cause brooks, streams, and rivers to run full all the time, and the temperature is kept so near in equilibrium, that storms cannot occur. And one can see that the pressure of the atmosphere is so much greater on the inside than on the outside world that lung trouble never affects the people, and no rank vegetation decays, and no malaria or bilious fevers arise, and ague never afflicts the people. The climates are almost antipodal to those on the exterior world. On the outer world, from the verge trending southward, is the coldest part, and icebergs and ice fields form and cover

1085

THE HIDDEN WORLD

the Asiatic and American shores between 60 and 80 degrees of what is called the Arctic regions.

It is a part of history that only a few hardy adventurers, navigators, or explorers, have ever passed through the ice belt, to catch sight of the open polar sea, to feel the warm airs or inhale the odors of sweet, strange flowers, from the the interior world. On the outer crust, southward, we encounter the temperate regions. After we leave the frigid, and still south of the temperate we meet the torrid zone or the equator, which is the warmest part of the exterior world, and then south of this is found the same climate as at the north, down to the southern verge.

As soon as the traveler fairly crosses the verge, and commences to enter into the inner crust, the climate grows warmer and warmer, and when fairly within the verge, and beneath what is termed the Arctic zone on the outer world the climate becomes tropical. The reason for this is evident. First, because the heat of the great electric belt is immediately felt, and no lands of ice, snow, or frost ever send their chilling blasts, like those prevailing upon the blustering and changeable exterior world. And second, because the sun, pouring his unobstructed rays into the great opening, three thousand miles in circumference, strikes the crust of the inner world, and then is reflected back and forth upon the hills, mountains, precipices, rivers, lakes, and oceans, thus getting the full benefit of reflected and refracted rays of light, such as the outer world never gets. While the constant light and heat of the great electrical belt never ceases, night or day, and while it is less, of course, than the heat of the sun, it always prevails, and its everlasting continuous heat gives perpetual warmth to the inner world.

The atmosphere being more dense, and unvexed by hurricanes, hail-storms, or tornadoes, retains the gentle heat, which does not pass off so readily by radiation. And one can see by the position of the inner earth to the sun, that at all seasons of the year the sun is shining always in at the north or south opening, and there is everlasting daylight, and everlasting electrical sunshine, to keep up this tropical climate over all that part of the inner world reached by the rays of the sun, where there is no night; and this with the electrical belt, would make an equatorial climate, on the inner world, corresponding to the arctic climate on the exterior world. As you penetrate deeper toward the inner world, the rays of the sun are less direct. They furnish less heat, and the climate for the first time becomes cooler, and corresponds with the temperate climate of the exterior world. And so in both worlds, the temperate is the zone best adapted for man's habitation.

From what has been said the conclusion naturally follows, that the center of the inner world would be an arctic climate, as it is shut off from the direct rays of the sun, and it would become the exact antipodes of the tropical center of the exterior world, blazing under the light of the direct rays of the sun.

This would be true, but certain conditions cause the geographical center of the inner world to have a climate of unparalleled excellence, partaking of a true mean, having combined in it the best features of the exterior world.

No storms ever convulse its tranquil atmosphere.

Its remoteness from the openings, at either end of the world, shut off the direct rays of the outer sun, protecting it from the vicissitudes of day and night, as in the changing seasons of the exterior world. It is located between the two temperate zones, north and south, inheriting from them the best climatic influences.

And the great globe, or electrical sun, gives a constant, unchanging, and unvarying heat, adapted to perfect health, and the ideal perfection of its vegetable, arboreal, and animal life. No droughts, no wet seasons, no changing moons, ever disturb its perfect climate.

For this is the land of the Happy Isle, which mankind have always dreamed about, and have tried in vain to find.

Man cannot eliminate from his mind some fair country which meets the requirements of his unsatisfied nature.

Hence the daring soul sought among the flowers of Florida the Fountain of Youth, others the Valhalla and Hesperides, somewhere in the mysterious seas of the west.

1087

THE HIDDEN WORLD

As the reader already knows, this Happy Isle was surrounded by water, in the midst of the oceans, pouring their multitudinous floods from all lands into that awful chasm, ten thousand miles in circumference, and whose prodigious cataracts created by their convulsions, the electricity for the light of the inner world, the electric sun, the electrical belt, and the aurora borealis, at the north and south extremities of the earth. The amount of electricity was such that the air, over the Happy Isle, looked like diamond dust, and it toned up all animal and vegetable life, so that flowers, and men and women, looked radiant and bright beyond the power of description.

This island was a thousand miles in diameter, just the size of the openings in the earth. In the center was a lofty mountain, white as alabaster, named Mount Zion, where the ark of the covenant found a final resting-place until the recall to Jerusalem occurs.

The summit of the mountain is miles across. And a mighty fountain of water spouts up into the air a vast distance, and falling in a circle, flows down the mountain side, and runs off in a thousand clear beautiful streams, in all directions to water the Happy Isle.

This water is clear as crystal and cures all diseases. Goldfish sport through its sparkling waters. Birds of gorgeous and brilliant plumage fly through its ambient air. Sea fowls, snowy white, glide over the pellucid waters, that for a hundred miles out from the shores shine like a sea of tranquil silver. Far out where the thundering waters pour into the gulf a mist rises towards the heavens, and the whole sky is surrounded by brilliant rainbows, presenting a spectacle of enchanting and indescribable splendor. Sparkling rays of electric light mounts up to the central orb which supplies light and heat for all the inner world, and shooting out on the electric belt, gives light and heat to the temperate and tropical land, and flowing out at the openings, makes the mysterious white light so perpetually seen at the poles, and the aurora borealis are streaming off through space and, united with the sun, they hold the earth firmly in position.

1088

Countries of large extent and royal beauty spread over the Happy Isle. The people walk daily with God and live in paradistic pleasures. Every tree and shrub produces bud, blossom, flower, and fruit, like Paradise before the fall at Eden. Indeed some of the Rabbis say the inner world was Paradise, and at the fall Adam and Eve were driven out of the inner world, on to the bleak outer world of thistles and thorns, of cold and heat, and with the passions of their evil natures they have turned it to a veritable land of Abaddon.

In the Happy Isle nothing grows in vain.

Under the instructions of their wisest men, they have obtained such a knowledge in chemistry and the laws of nature that they can produce any food they want, and they are independent of the slavish labor imposed upon men on the outer world.

He who keeps up with the progress of events on the outer world will see that men there have caught an inkling of the possibilities of science, and I append below an article cut from the editorial of the Indianapolis Daily Journal of September, 1894, which reads as follows:

"An article in one of the September magazines treating of the possibilities of science in the near future, quotes a noted French chemist as expressing the opinion that chemistry will eventually displace agriculture in supplying food. Chemists have already succeeded in making fat direct from its elements. If fat, why not lean? and these given, why may not chemistry produce the equivalent of beefsteak? Perhaps the product might not be as toothsome or juicy as steak, and probably it would never supplant the latter in the estimation of old, fastidious gourmands. But the coming man, he of the twentieth century, may not be an old-fashioned gourmand. He may be so thoroughly utilitarian, and withal so busy, that he will not care what he eats, so that it shall sustain life and furnish the necessary fuel for brain and body. Who knows but the coming man may eat meat, eggs, milk and other foods in the form of tablets, swallowing his dessert in capsules, and top off with a glass of wine, in the shape of a pill? It is a fact, by the way, that one of the chemical products of coal tar is saccharine, a perfect

1089

substitute for sugar, except that it is forty times as sweet, an ounce of it furnishing more sweetening matter than three pounds of the purest sugar."

No domestic animals are ever seen on the Happy Isle, and all calls for animal food is met by chemical processes, but the wonderful food-supply of nature is such on the Happy Isle, that the bloody spectacle of a butcher's shop and the taking of animal life is never seen. No Hebrew under eighty years of age is a legal candidate to enter the Happy Isle, that age being fixed as the maximum age, when the wisdom of experience and the spiritual development has ripened sufficient to become a full-fledged candidate for admission. Occasionally there are persons of such extraordinary spiritual endowments and who have led a life so just and pure for years, that the Mirror of God discloses no blemish or stain as they stand before it. For such a person a dispensation can be procured. None ever die on the Happy Isle as they die on the exterior world; they simply go to sleep and lie on the side of Mount Zion, awaiting the call of the Resurrection trumpet at the Millennium. They are like one of old who declared he should see God in the flesh. None ever go to sleep under 420 years, and they spend their time in studying science, religion, the philosophy of life, the structure and essence of matter, and intellectual and spiritual development. Some study the laws of life, analyze the elements, and when they master them they go out to the Himalaya Mountains, become Mahatmas, who sometimes make themselves known to mortals of superior discernment and development. In a few words, they live such a life as God intended for Adam and Eve in the garden before their disobedience and transgression. Once a year the Great White Ship sailed to the mainland and brought to the Happy Isle the righteous Jews, whose life permitted them to emigrate thither. There was no free importation of sinners allowed, no free emigration, permitted by the laws of God. A blameless life was the passport which He ordained for entrance to the Happy Isle.

Near Anderson, Indiana, the home of the author, some four miles up White River from the beautiful city, near the

Anderson Mounds, on which the remains of the prehistoric race called the Mound Builders can be seen, is a high bluff, near these mouldering earthworks of an extinct people. At the foot of this bluff White River flows, and on the side of the steep bluff is a spring, from which flows a water of peculiar taste and medicinal qualities, and on the low hills of the Happy Isle, which rise near the mysterious sea, and run to Mount Zion, in the center of the Happy Isle, there is a spring like that at Anderson, which is called the Pool of Siloam. These hills rise gradually till they assume proportions like those of Galilee, and about fifty miles from Mount Zion there is a valley, not far from this pool, and in this valley flows a bright little stream, and on the side of the hill is a city, which, in memory of their fatherland, the Jews in the Happy Isle called "Nazareth", and once a year this celebrated city is painted or photographed on the skies of the outer world, and is seen suspended in the air over Glacier Bay, in Alaska.

We do not profess to understand the whys and the wherefores of those mirages often seen in deserts and on the ocean.

But the aerial city of Nazareth has been seen so often, that I call attention to it by citing below a cutting from the Indianapolis Journal. Why it should only happen once a year, and after the fullmoon; is a mystery, but if you will consult the position of the moon, the sun, and the earth, at the full of the moon, in June, you will see it is the only time in the year when the open space, in front of the Happy Isle, could possibly be seen and reflected on the sky out of the north opening, and it happens to be when the Mirror of God is being used to test the purity of the Jews who aspire to go to the Happy Isle. We leave the problem to be solved by the inquisitive, to suit their own opinions.

"PERHAPS IT IS HEAVEN."

"Beautiful city seen suspended in the air over Glacier Bay, Alaska.

"TACOMA, WASH., June 26, 1894. - A suspended city has
1091

THE HIDDEN WORLD

CITY SEEN IN THE SKY ABOVE THE VERGE.

THE HIDDEN WORLD

been discovered off Glacier Bay, Alaska, by a party of excursionists. This curious phenomenon is seen regularly after the full moon in June, and at no other time. It is declared to be a beautiful mirage of some unknown city suspended in the rarefied air directly over the bay. A photographer has taken pictures of it four times, but so far no one has been able to identify a single one of the ghostly buildings outlined in its plates."

While this little Jewish city of Nazareth has been immortalized in the world as the residence of Christ, it is a significant and romantic event that once a year, the planets in the sky and the elements conspire to reproduce it in the air of the outer world, and although hidden in the center of the earth, once a year God paints it on the northern sky and thus draws aside the veil, to remind mankind of Him who drew aside the veil of death and made resurrection possible for the doomed posterity of Adam.

On various occasions the heavens have exhibited such supernatural appearances, that they were conjectured by some to foreshadow coming, or existing events.

"September 16, 1837, at Berwick, in Scotland, the gigantic British Lion, with forepaws extended, was quietly suppressing the grim likeness of Mr. Parnell; on the left was a large harp, on the right the head of the Queen.

"In 1683, when Vienna was relieved by Sobieski, and the Turks were finally driven from Europe, a sword and reversed crescent were seen in the sky.

"On the eve of the battle of Culloden, King George II and his family, at Windsor, beheld in the clouds the thistles of Scotland reversed, and the outline of a Highlander, armed with a claymore and targe falling backwards.

"The Emperor Constantine, in one of his marches above the meridian sun, saw the luminous cross inscribed with these words: 'By this conquer.' And this was seen by the whole army.

"Charlemagne saw bands of soldiers struggling in the skies. The Crusaders saw saints and martyrs in the sky, mounted on white horses."

We leave the beautiful city of Nazareth, suspended in the

1093

air over Glacier Bay, for the consideration of the reader, to make much or little of it, as his ideas of the natural or supernatural may dictate.

CHAPTER XV.

BEN HUSA AND NARDO.

BEN HUSA, of the tribe of Benjamin, had been the lover of Rebecca before she knew Nardo. While she had not encouraged his advances, he was received by the family with respect, for he was a leading Pharisee. He was proud of his lineage, cold, austere, reserved, religious, and controversial. When Rebecca manifested a preference for Nardo, it aroused all of the animosity which jealousy inspires and religious begotry creates.

To think that a theathen, a barbarous Chickimec, should find more favor in the eyes of the peerless Jewess, was the sum of impudence, and he resolved to humiliate Nardo as soon as possible.

He misconstrued all that Nardo said. He criticised all his acts as foolish, illiberal, and especially condemned him because he was known as a follower of Christ, whom the Jews rejected.

He charged Nardo with heresy, with being a follower of Christ, and a teacher of strange and dangerous doctrines, and encountering Nardo on one occasion, when several Jewish Doctors, Pharisees, and Rabbis were present, he considered that his opportunity had come; he therefore accosted Nardo, and said:

"Nardo, it you will persist in regarding Christ as the Messiah, for the sake of Jehovah quit teaching the doctrine of the trinity, for of all the absurd, illogical, unnatural, and detestable things the trinity is the most contemptible."

Nardo said: "Why, Ben Husa, you are quite personal and very severe on the trinity today."

"No more so than it, or they, as the case may be, deserve. There is nothing in nature, philosophy, or religion, to sustain the absurd idea of Father, Son, and Holy Ghost,

1094

THE HIDDEN WORLD

three in one. And Ben Husa sneered contemptuously and looked proudly towards the Doctors and others for their approbation.

The color heightened in Nardo's cheeks; his eyes shone, but with a great effort to restrain his rising indignation, he replied:

"Ben Husa, without noticing your sneer, or caring for it, I beg leave to take issue with your statement, that there is nothing 'in nature, philosophy, or religion, to sustain the idea of a trinity,' for I hold that nature abounds with the ideas of trinity in almost all important things."

"Well, well," said Ben Husa, "we would be delighted to have one poor evidence of a trinity, three in one, and I am certain nature, which you say 'is full of trinity,' will not be burdened with carrying all Trinitarian ideas. We await the disclosure of the learned Rabbi, Sir Trinitarian Nardo."

Without noting the sarcasm of Ben Husa, Nardo said:

"We have earth, air, and sky. Water, ice, and frost, three in one. Man is of the flesh, intellect, and spirit; he has head, body, and limbs. His feet have joints in his toes, ankle, and foot. He has joint in his hips, knees, and feet. Each finger has three joints. He has joints at the wrist, elbow, and shoulder. Joints in the neck, backbone, and hips. He has infancy, maturity, and old age. He has a birth, life, and death. His cradle, bed, and his coffin. A father, mother, and God. He is a Trinitarian from the cradle to his grave.

"Looking from man to a tree, we see root, tree, and bark. The heart, body, and bark. The tree has leaf, blossom, and fruit. The nut has seed, flesh, and skin. The weed has root, stem, and pistil. The seed germinates in the ground, grows in the air, and ripens in the sun. The Scripture teaches that we have Father, Son, and Holy Ghost. The air blows and proclaims the trinity; the waves flow in a trinity, each breath of wind, and each wave that beats the shore, blows, and beats, so that each third one is louder, and heavier than its two predecessors. We have earth, moon, and sun. Water, earth, and air. Ears, eyes, and mouth, to hear, see, and speak. Men, angels, and God.

"In your creed, you have God and the Messiah, two in

1095

one. We have Father, Son, and Holy Ghost, three in one, just as water has three in one, for water becomes frost, ice, and snow, three in one. And taking nature as a guide, a trinity is the order of the universe, and so, I say, nature everywhere is full of trinity, three in one."

"Well, I declare," said Ben Husa, "you make a formidable showing of the trinity, I must admit."

"Indeed he does," spoke up three of the Doctors at one time, and one of the Pharisees, who said:

"Ben Husa, you will have to surrender," and there was a general laugh at Ben Husa's expense. Ben Husa rallied as quick as he could and said:

"Whatever Nardo may say about the trinity, we all know that when our Messiah is come, there is to be a resurrection of the body, and that has never occurred, and so Nardo must admit that his Christ is not our Messiah, for when He comes there is to be a general resurrection of the dead, and the dominion of death is to be broken, and as that has not come, Nardo must admit that his Christ is a failure, an impostor, and the Messiah has not come."

"No, indeed," said Nardo, "I don't admit any such thing, but I fearlessly assert that in Christ we have seen the fulfillment of this prophecy in toto."

"How can that be?" exclaimed Ben Husa and all the Doctors, and a Pharisee said:

"In toto! impossible. Not only impossible, but Nardo cannot give any satisfactory evidence of such an incredible thing."

"Reverend Fathers in Israel, I feel certain of your attention, and I only ask a fair hearing while I offer proofs, or rather while I offer evidence."

"We will listen for evidence or proofs. We will not even argue, your statement seems so preposterous and incredible."

"Well, then, you all remember that for their transgression in Eden, Adam and Eve were doomed to death, not a mere temporal physical death, but an everlasting death of body and spirit; that when they descended to the grave, it was eternal death to them and their seed. But even in that

1096

THE HIDDEN WORLD

dreadful hour there was a prophecy of redemption, and as man went to the grave to abide there, they continued to die for centuries, until Christ came; the dominion of death continued unbroken. It became necessary that Christ should die, and so He was crucified, but arose the third day, never to come under the dominion of death again. Thus He became the first-fruits of the resurrection, and He gave to the earth a resurrection power, and through Him all men are to be resurrected. Thus is seen the general resurrection of the dead has occurred in toto. Had it not been for the resurrection of Christ, no man could have been resurrected. Now all men can be, and so I say the resurrection of all men has occurred.

"These things all have come before the appearance of your expected Messiah. And I think you misconstrue the resurrection, in supposing that your Messiah is going to resurrect all the dead; but the proper construction should be, that Christ, in His resurrection, was a type of the ultimate resurrection of all men from the dominion of death.

"But whether correct or not in this connection, as bearing on the trinity as well as the resurrection, you will remember that at the day of Pentecost what is recorded in the sacred parchment, is as follows:

" 'Suddenly there came a sound from heaven, as of a rushing mighty wind, and it filled all the house. And there appeared unto them cloven tongues like as of fire, and it sat upon each of them. And they were all filled with the HOLY GHOST, and began to speak with other tongues, as the Spirit gave them utterance. And there were present devout men from every nation under heaven. And they were all amazed, and marvelled, saying one to another: Behold, are not all these Galileans? And how hear we every man in our own tongue, wherein we were born? Parthians, Medes, and Elamites, and dwellers in Mesopotamia, and in Judaea, and Cappadocia, in Pontus, Asia, Phrygia, Pamphylia, in Egypt, and in parts of Lydia, about Cyrene, and strangers of Rome, Jews, and proselytes, Cretes, and Arabians.' Acts 2:2-11.

"You will discover in this quotation from the sacred book, that more nations and more witnesses were present

1097

THE HIDDEN WORLD

at this wonderful scene than of any other transaction in the world. Also your particular attention is called to the fact that the words SPIRIT and HOLY GHOST, are especially mentioned. Here then we have historic evidence of two parties of the trinity. Many had seen Christ while living - some after His resurrection, and all were witnesses of the HOLY GHOST, sitting as cloven tongues of fire - all heard the rushing mighty wind. And so I claim that here is an undisputed proof of the SON and HOLY GHOST, two out of the three, in the trinity, and no one questions the existence of the FATHER, and so I claim to have given solid proofs of the trinity and of the general resurrection."

"But then," said Ben Husa, "we all know that when the Messiah comes, He is to be with the people in person for a thousand years; your facts don't clear that objection."

"But, Ben Husa," said Nardo, "you fail to remember that is to be at the second coming of Christ, it is not predicted of His first, but His second coming, at the Millennium."

"Oh, there is where you crawl out, Sir Nardo."

"I don't crawl, Ben Husa; it is what the Scripture teaches."

"Well," responded Ben Husa, "you seem so conversant with the Scriptures, with the trinity, and the resurrection, you perhaps can explain the other prophecy. About 'a temple, erected which shall not be destroyed, and one King over the earth. The temple at Jerusalem has been destroyed, and there is to be but one King over the earth.' I suppose you can crack that nut for us as flippantly as you think you have the trinity and resurrection," and Ben Husa looked around triumphantly, and apparently for approbation.

"Yes, yes," said the Doctors and the Pharisees, "the temple that is never to be destroyed and the one King."

"To me," replied Nardo, "it is as easy as the others, but you may not see it as I do."

"Oh, yes, we will all see when we have such a learned Rabbi as Sir Nardo, who rattles off prophecy like water from a duck's back," sneered Ben Husa.

"To all fair-minded men I'm willing to give the best

1098

rendering of the Scriptures I can, but to a sneering son of Abaddon, I don't care to talk."

"Abaddon!" cried Ben Husa, "Abaddon! that means a son of perdition."

"So I understand," was the freezing reply of Nardo.

"Abaddon! You shall repent in sackcloth and ashes for this insult!" hotly said Ben Husa.

"Ben Husa, your conduct has been ungenerous, your sneers uncalled for, your threats I defy, but for these Doctors and Pharisees, I respect them - and to you, gentlemen, I will give my explanation, but from henceforth I shall not recognize Ben Husa as one of my auditors."

"No, oh, no, a smart proselyte is of more consequence, in his own estimation, than one who can trace his genealogy directly to Abraham."

Without paying the least attention to Ben Husa, Nardo, addressing himself directly to the others, said:

"Men of Israel, by the temple I do not understand a temple such as Titus destroyed, but, as I understand it, the temple means man. That man is a temple in which God dwells. Between Adam and Christ, the temple or man had been destroyed by the sentence of death at Eden. When Christ came and was resurrected He resurrected a temple, and made man immortal after His resurrection, and man is the temple which is never to be destroyed, a temple in which God's Spirit shall dwell forever, and so the resurrection of man is the temple which is never to be destroyed."

"That is a plausible idea, and it is not without force, for we all hope for eternal life, and immortality is an attractive thing, but," said Montader, a Pharisee, "how about the one King over the earth?"

"Oh," said Nardo, "if Christ is conqueror over death and the grave, is He not the only King over all the earth? In that sense He is - but in a wider sense do you not believe and expect that the Jewish Messiah when he comes will be King over all the earth. You certainly do, and the believers in Christ expect His kingdom to be all over the earth. And we claim that at the atonement, when the Comforter and the Holy Ghost come, that they leaven all the world, and then

1099

there will be but one King."

"I must say," replied the Pharisee, "that I don't feel inclined at this time to controvert what you have so graphically put."

"Men of Israel, you will remember that Joel said:

" 'I will pour out my Spirit upon all flesh, and your sons and your daughters shall prophesy, and your young men shall see visions, and your old men shall dream dreams.' " - Acts 2:17.

" 'And righteousness and peace shall cover the earth, as the waters cover the sea,' and if that does not establish one King, I fail to comprehend the prophecies."

"We will admit your statements are not without force; but all Israel believe that, before the Messiah, Elijah is to come, and all war is to cease."

"Very good. But in John the Baptist we recognize Elijah in appearance and teaching. He went before Christ, preaching in the wilderness and proclaiming Him. He baptized with water, but Christ with a baptism of fire, such as Moses saw in the burning bush, and such as was seen at the Pentecost. And, as for peace, you recollect that the whole world looked for the coming of Christ; and, for the first time since creation, the temple of Janus was closed, and there was peace throughout the whole world. And the angels who spoke to the shepherds said: 'Peace on earth, and good will to men.' It is nowhere asserted that no war shall follow after Christ appeared. Indeed, He teaches that He brings a sword; not a carnal weapon, but the sword of the Spirit, and this shall continue until the whole world, except Anti-Christ, is converted; and when it believes in Him, there will be peace and one King, Christ Jesus. As He stilled the tempest, and calmed the waves of Galilee, so shall He speak peace to every tempest-tossed sinner's soul. In a spiritual sense, therefore, He gives peace to all His followers; and while He fills them with indescribable love, they necessarily are at peace with God and man. While He reigns in their hearts He brings peace, not war, and He becomes the one King over all the earth. And I think no one will doubt that He is King over the Christian world."

1100

"Well, Nardo," said the Pharisee, "for a proselyte, and not a born Jew, you speak wonderful words of wisdom; but if all you say is true, or a portion of it, I cannot see why Jehovah should send the Ten Tribes to the inside of the world, and erect an icy barrier south of the verge to forever hide us from the outer world."

"If you will recall what Jeremiah says in chapter xvi., verses 14,15, you will discover a reason, where he says: 'It shall no more be said, The Lord liveth that brought up the children of Israel out of the land of Egypt, but the Lord liveth that brought up the children of Israel from the North, and from all the lands whither He hath driven them, and I will bring them again unto their land that I gave their fathers.' And Isaiah tells us that the children of Israel shall come from 'the isles of the west' (from the word yam, meaning all towards the sun setting); that is, the Jews who at present inhabit a certain part of America, but are concealed in the extremities of the earth. And you remember that Rabbi Akiba observes 'that as the days pass on and never return, so these tribes have also passed away, and may never be expected to come back.' 'Lo, the people shall dwell alone, and shall not be reckoned among nations.' (Ibid., 219). And Zachariah says in chapter xiv., 9, 'And the Lord shall be King over all the earth. In that day the Lord alone shall be acknowledged, and His name shall also be one.' 'And the earth shall be full of all sorts of science and wisdom, which shall cause tranquillity, and there shall be no jealousy one of another, nor ambition one of another, but peace in all the universe.' (River Sombatyon, p. 272.) To be brief, and save further proof, the Lord has sent you here that the Scriptures might be fulfilled about a return from the Northland, and to show all the world His care for His chosen people. If we hope for the redemption, and this return to Jerusalem, we must make ourselves worthy of it, and by heroic work, and unflagging patience, and Abrahamic faith, accept the good, reject the evil, and become as pure-hearted as the priest who goes barefooted once a year, and once in his lifetime only, into the Holy of Holies, and from the Urim and Thummim learns the will of Jehovah."

1101

THE HIDDEN WORLD

THE WHITE SHIP AND GOLDEN MIRROR.

A, Golden Gate. B, Mirror of God. C, Platform. D, Path of approach
E, Path of accepted. F, Path of rejected. G, Holy Ground.
H, White Ship. I, Wall. J, Mysterious Sea.

1102

"Learn the will of fiddlesticks! Impostor, cunning charlatan, and hypocritical Chickimec, I've enough of your balderdash;" and with a clinched fist Ben Husa advanced close to Nardo and spat in his face.

It was too much for Chickimec blood to bear, and, without stopping to check his rising anger, Nardo knocked Ben Husa down, and recovering himself, he said: "Men of Israel, it was too insulting; it came so sudden. I beg your pardon." And with folded arms he stood while Ben Husa was lifted to his feet.

Ben Husa glared at him, wiped the blood from his face, and said: "Your doom is sealed."

"God alone seals our doom. 'As ye sow, so shall ye reap,'" said Nardo; and turning, he deliberately walked away.

And thus closed this contest of creeds and beliefs, as they have so often done in the history of man, with violence and blood.

CHAPTER XVI.

THE GOLDEN GATE, THE MIRROR OF GOD, THE GREAT WHITE SHIP, AND THE HAPPY ISLE.

THE Scriptures tell us that God tries with His reins every human heart. That as the heart is, so is the man. That God's unerring eye looks into the secrets of every heart, and while man cannot see the secret spring, God does. That while man's spirit is shrined in a tabernacle of flesh, and subject to its carnal desires, the Spirit strives with celestial aim to teach man his higher destiny, to illumine his soul, and lift man to a loftier plane. Many believe there will come a time, after death and resurrection, when man shall stand before the eye of God, with the veil withdrawn, and his whole life exposed.

If such be the case in the Jewish history, men have so stood in God's presence and lived. The high-priest dared not enter the Holy of Holies except he was pure within and without.

THE HIDDEN WORLD

When Moses came down from the Mount, he had been before God; he had been purified from all sin, and his face shone with a brightness which no man could look upon until his face was covered with a veil.

While these rare displays are "like angels' visits, few and far between," no reason can be given why, when the cloud and pillar of fire had conducted His children into the hidden world, and a barrier of eternal ice had been erected by an immutable law, to keep the world away, He should not give to them occasional reminders of His providential and continuous care.

In the Golden Gate, in the Mirror of God, in the Sacred Ground, and in the Great White Ship, we have reminders of God's care as encouragement to keep the faith of the Lost Tribes unchanged until the time comes for their return to Jerusalem.

By the direction of Melchisedec a high wall had been built. Across the peninsula, which extended into the mysterious sea, the Golden Gate hung. An archway was built for the Mirror of God, and when men stood before the mirror, they could see themselves as out of God's eyes, something similar to the high-priest, when he consulted the URIM and THUMMIM, once a year, in the Holy of Holies.

The Golden Gate was always shut except once a year, when the White Ship came for those who could stand the test before the Mirror of God, and closed as soon as they had crossed the portal.

The Mirror had been erected by Melchisedec, and reflected with fidelity the forms of all who looked upon it the year round, except when the annual test came, when it glowed with a brilliancy so intense, that only those whom God approved could look into it; and then they saw the secrets of their own hearts, and a soul free from spot or blemish, and while filled with a divine joy and happiness, which the redeemed feel, they were borne with resistless power through the Golden Gate, which opened and closed noiselessly, and they were presently on the White Ship, which was of spotless purity and snowy loveliness.

Before the mirror was the platform on which the person

1104

stood. If their life was impure they could not look upon the mirror, for their sin, black and horrible, confronted them, and a powerful force pushed them off the platform, faced them outwards, onto the pathway, and their mortal fear made them hasten away, resolved to correct their life, during the year, and abandon the sin, which they saw clearly reflected upon the mirror, and this with a quickened conscience, would generally lead them into a proper life. It is all the time to be recollected that none but those over eighty years of age ever undertook the test, and those who were renowned for their honesty, purity, charity, and Christian graces generally. There was, however, an exception to those of younger age, if they were persons of great spiritual endowment, and whose life was full of good works, and those approved by the Sanhedrin, and of Jewish birth, or licensed by a permit from the high-priest.

Here is seen the sacred ground, and no one ever dared to put a foot upon this ground, for they were forced back by a strong power, and if they did not leave, they were hurled away, and thrown upon the ground with such violence that no one ever attempted it again. Melchisedec informed them that a second attempt would be death. And they had seen so many displays of power during their pilgrimage, that none attempted it a second time.

The one thing about the White Ship which seemed unexplainable, was that they could not see the power which impelled it through the water. No steam, no oars, no wind seemed to do it, for it always came, when the sea was smooth, and the sky was clear, and no wind blowing. And it was never seen except once a year, and when all the accepted were on board it moved around and sailed away as mysteriously as it came, and was not visible again until the next year. Only Melchisedec seemed to understand it. In a work as restricted as this, a great many things must be omitted, and only the thread of the life and events connected with the history of the principal characters can be noted. And this chapter will narrate events that happened to those referred to ten years after the close of last chapter. Melchisedec had come and gone year after year, with the

1105

White Ship, and Ben Husa had persecuted Nardo in every possible manner. He had fostered a spirit, among those of the seed of Abraham, and a strong following had sprung up of antipathy to Gentiles and foreigners, and the Sanhedrin, composed mainly of Pharisees, had enacted a law that no heathen could marry a Jew or Jewess, until after ten years' residence among them, and not then until a dispensation had been granted by the high-priest, and the influence of Ben Husa had kept the marriage of Nardo and Rebecca from being solemnized for ten years, who could not get a dispensation, and to escape this persecution, they had agreed together to present themselves before the Mirror of God, and, if accepted, sail away to the Happy Isle, and thus promote their happiness, and escape from this long and aggravated persecution.

And now, having made these explanations, we are prepared for the following events:

The light disclosed the tenth return of the White Ship, with her snow sails resting like a thing of beauty upon the glassy surface of the mysterious sea.

The Golden Gate glowed with unwonted splendor, the Mirror of God blazed and threw out a strong beam of light in front and far away, more brilliant and of more intense and penetrating power than anything they had ever seen.

There was no heat in it, simply light; it made the pebbles glitter like gems wherever it touched them, the grass, flowers, and trees shone like burnished silver. The limbs of trees and trunks seemed to be solid silver, the stems of the leaves like silver veins, and the leaves, as they rose and fell and waved in the breeze, presented a flashing splendor which no language can portray.

It is needless to say that all who witnessed this remarkable scene were wonderfully impressed, and a subdued and reverential feeling pervaded all hearts. This is a common feeling when men believe themselves in the presence of God.

The Golden Gate swung open, and Melchisedec, dressed in pure white, advanced through it, and seated himself upon a chair as white as alabaster. The gate then closed, and,

1106

waving his hand, he signaled for those to appear who were candidates for the Happy Isle to advance and test their blameless life and character. Music, soft and sweet as that which floats on the air when the low AEolian harp strings vibrate from some bower of beauty, swelled out from the snowy sails of the White Ship and filled all hearts with the charm of heaven-inspired melody. When the waiting thousands recognized the well-known and venerable Melchisedec they were in some sense reassured, and one by one the pious and aged sons of Israel advanced with their wives, and stopping on the platform, looked into the Mirror of God, which no one dared to face who did not feel, or fancy they felt, at peace with God and man. The first to advance was Rabbi Joseph, named after him of Egypt, and partaking of that purity of mind and heart which has made the Joseph of Potiphar the one unique and renowned character of all ages; and as Rabbi Joseph looked into the mirror, having the peace of God in his soul, he saw a heart as white as the most pellucid alabaster, and in his hand a stone, with a new name written in it, unknown to all but God and himself, and his spirit, so spotless and pure, that not one stain of earth, time or carnality cast on it an infinitesimal shade.

The Golden Gate swung open, and with a soul flowing with love and thankfulness, he and his wife passed through it and on to the White Ship. The gate closed, and Rabbi Ben Alonzo and wife Naomi advanced and saw what Rabbi Joseph did, and he and his wife were received in the same manner. Man after man was accepted, until Pharisee Esder Olam stepped upon the platform, when he suddenly threw up his hands, wheeled to the right, and hurried over the pathway of the rejected. None knew what he saw; all believed there was some secret sin hid from the eye of man, but revealed to that of God, and in this public manner seen by the rejected Pharisee. The test continued from day to day until all of the men of eighty had been tested and accepted or rejected, and the time came for Rebecca and Nardo, and we will now give our attention to them.

Rebecca advanced first, while Nardo tarried behind, some distance in the rear of Melchisedec, leaving Rebecca, as it

1107

was the custom for the maidens to go alone. Now Rebecca, robed in pure white, with her hair black as the raven's plume, with a bunch of flowers upon her breast, white as her own lovely soul, and with a crimsoned band around her waist, holding her snowy drapery to her symmetrical person, with a face beaming with happiness and radiant with love, and at peace with God and man, ascended the platform of test.

What she saw we leave to the reader to imagine, from one of her noble character and superior spiritual endowment; but her face took on a look which human language cannot describe, and, beaming with indescribable happiness, she glided along the pathway of the accepted, the Golden Gate swung wide open, and just as it was swinging to she glanced backwards, waved her hand to Nardo, showing that earth had yet its attraction, and she disappeared with a smile which an angel could not surpass for sweetness and trusting love.

Nardo immediately started along the pathway of approach, but he was arrested at the third step by a hand upon his shoulder, and turning, to his amazement he saw an officer with a warrant for his arrest for leaving without a permit from the high-priest, for he was still counted a heathen by Ben Husa and his followers.

Astonished at this detention, for he had been many more years than ten a proselyte, and had been adopted by their religious and civil polity, Nardo said:

"Who prefers this charge, now and here, where I am submitting to the test before the Mirror of God? By residence and adoption, I need no certificate or permit. The time, the place, the occasion; there is no precedent, no jurisdiction for the temporal laws of man to interfere before the tribunal of God, and the test of Jehovah. I demand to be permitted to proceed!"

"All times, places, jurisdictions, are proper for a heathen dog!" exclaimed Ben Husa, stepping from behind the officer. "Hold the scoundrel, and take him before the Sanhedrin. I told you you had sealed your doom."

Nardo had been so intently watching Rebecca, that he had

1108

not noticed the approach of Ben Husa and the officer, and, surprised and indignant, he said:

"You, Ben Husa! how dare you -" and before he could finish the sentence, Melchisedec turned, recognized Nardo, and waving to the officer and Ben Husa, he said:

"Back! back for your lives! you are in the presence of Jehovah!" With a pallid countenance the officer released Nardo and hurried away, but Ben Husa sprang in front of Nardo and said:

"In the name of the high-priest, the Sanhedrin, and Abraham, I command this heathen to stop."

Nardo, with a face blazing with anger, drew back his clinched hand, but before he could strike, Melchisedec said:

"Let justice be done."

Instantly Ben Husa was smitten as with a thunderbolt; he was hurled head-first clear beyond the retreating officer, and when picked up was dead.

Melchisedec called to Nardo to come to him, and said:

"Nardo, I fear the result of this unfortunate affair; will you try the test?"

"By all my hopes of heaven yes! Rebecca is yonder, beyond the Golden Gate; I'll go if I die!"

"Rash youth, beware; if rejected, don't you dare to resist. Remember Ben Husa. God be with you! Advance!"

Accordingly Nardo started, trying to compose himself, but when he mounted the platform, and looked into the mirror, he saw a black spot over his heart, a clouded stain around his spirit; an icy cold blast struck him, an all-powerful force gently pressed him back towards the path of the rejected, turned him around and with a cry of "Rebecca! my God!" he gave way and yielded to a power he dared not resist. When he returned to Melchisedec, he said:

"O Jehovah! I can't stand this! Rebecca! on the White Ship, bound for the Happy Isle, and I rejected by the mirror, and forced back to this horrible land. Oh, Melchisedec, can't you do something for me?"

"No, my son! no! Your anger towards Ben Husa would have carried sin to the Happy Isle. A heart harboring anger or a spirit of revenge can never enter there. What is a

1109

year to a young man like you? Rebecca is safe in the Happy Isle. She will learn why you did not come. I'll tell her that you will live a life of purity for a year. I'll bring her with me, here, next year on the White Ship, to meet you. Let me caution you to let no provocation or any human temptation ruffle your spirit or inflame your heart. Had you trusted to God, and not on yourself, Bén Husa would have met the fate he did. Had your spirit been as unruffled and your heart as pure as the matchless Rebecca, all would have been well, and you and she would have been on the White Ship and bound for the Happy Isle. Once more let me burn the lesson into your memory and engrave it on your heart, 'Justice is mine, saith the Lord, and I will repay.'

"My good, brave, gallant, and unfortunate friend Nardo, remember that the Lord can and will protect His own. Trust to Him, and all will be well."

"Melchisedec, my wise and noble mentor, I feel better, even now. I love God with all my heart, I can even now forgive Ben Husa, but, O Jehovah, how I love Rebecca!"

"Nardo, make not an idol of Rebecca; love God better than all, and next year you shall meet her never to part more in this life, provided you govern your spirit, for one who governs his own spirit 'is mightier than he who captures a city.' Keep therefore your heart pure and trust in God, not in an arm of flesh; trust the Infinite, not the finite. And now farewell; see, the women come."

At this moment a band of women, widows, and maidens, of blameless character, approached, and were tested, and rapidly admitted. Among these was a widow called Mara, and her daughter Ruth, who advanced together, and were duly admitted one by one. Mara in the Hebrew means sorrow or bitter, and while Mara had drained the cup of sorrow, she had trained Ruth so well that she was the social and religious equal of Rebecca, and between the two a great friendship and intimacy had sprung up. And when Mara and Ruth arrived on the White Ship, they saw Rebecca, with anxious and troubled countenance, looking wistfully back towards the Golden Gate for Nardo; but Ruth, running up and putting her arm around Rebecca, said:

1110

THE HIDDEN WORLD

"It was the fault of Ben Husa, but Ben Husa is dead. Nardo had no permit to marry from the high-priest. Ben Husa attempted to stop him. Nardo became angry and attempted to strike Ben Husa, but God did the striking. Ben Husa is dead. The anger of Nardo kept him out for this time, but he will come in next year, for Melchisedec said so, and he knows."

"What! did not Nardo stand the test? Impossible! I know his pure heart too well."

"Oh, yes," said Ruth. "His heart is pure, he gave way to anger, as Moses did. And he is kept out only for a year, but Moses was kept out always."

Overwhelmed with grief, Rebecca withdrew to herself, and in her heart she mused as follows:

"What is the Happy Isle to me without Nardo! What are its lovely skies, flowery vales, bright waters, and Elysian fields, while my heart is beyond the Golden Gate." But after a little time she composed her troubled spirit, and thought, "Hard as it may be, I must say, 'not my will, but Thine, be done.' Oh my sweetheart, you will be true, you will think of me, you will come in a year. I will be good, you'll be true, and when you come, God will give us a long and happy life.

"Have I made Nardo an idol? If so, God is teaching me a sore lesson. I will not repine and blame God, for He is good; 'twas the fault of Ben Husa, the hypocritical Pharisee, and maybe we did make idols of each other. O great Jehovah, in this dark hour I bow to Thy decree, and in this chastisement, I'll try to see a loving hand, I'll try to hope for the best, and, Lord, Thy will, not mine, be done."

Rebecca then grew calmer, and when night came she resigned herself to her couch, invoking Jehovah's kindest care for her lover, and fell into a dreamless sleep.

Meantime the test was continued from day to day, and many women, widows, and maidens, sometimes called old maids, were admitted, for it often happens that the cream of women never marry, but, like evangelists, bless the world with good deeds.

Among them were several namesakes of Biblical and

1111

historical characters, namely: Tamar, Galphyra, Atalia, Bathsheba, Bernice, Agrippa, Deborah, and Clodea, and many others we cannot take time to enumerate.

About this time the glorious light began to fade from the Mirror of God, and Melchisedec said to Nardo:

"See, the light is fading, and I must pass through the Golden Gate before the Mirror loses its last heavenly luster, for the gate will then close and not open for a year. Farewell and remember."

Melchisedec then passed slowly down the pathway of the accepted, and just before he went through the gate he saw Ruth with a package in her hand which she tossed to him saying:

"For Nardo."

Melchisedec turned, waved his hand towards Nardo, tossed something out which fell beyond the sacred ground, and Nardo picked it up and found the following lines in the beautiful handwriting of Rebecca.

REBECCA TO NARDO.

We met beneath the sun's red glare,
    But we are parted now;
Grief claims from each sad heart a sigh,
    O'erclouds each loving brow.

Tho' rolling seas and shores divide,
    And tears drop o'er the main,
We ask of dark futurity,
    When shall we meet again?

Oh, we shall meet, when fate's decree
    Has clarified thy soul,
Then loving eyes again shall see,
    Beyond where billows roll.

No gates of fate, no gates of gold,
    Can withstand the leaven,
For pure hearts and trusting love

1112

THE HIDDEN WORLD

    Will ope the gates of heaven.

Then live a life unknown to sin,
    Of grief and hate bereft,
Whose radiant spirit shows no stain
    Upon the Mirror left.

The Golden Gate swings free and wide,
    And white across the tide
The ship shall spread her snowy sail,
    To bring a joyous bride.

Wipe from thy heart each stain of hate
    Meet all with proud disdain,
Rebecca, with undying trust,
    Shall meet her love again.

Rebecca on the enchanting Isle,
    Nardo across the sea,
A dark eclipse is hanging o'er
    The fancy once so free.

Recall the faith of other days,
    Trust Jehovah for his grace,
And in his own appointed ways
    He'll bring us face to face.
                  Rebecca.

Nardo pressed the lines reverently to his lips, and said to himself, "Oh, the faith, the trust, the courage and the love of that blessed maiden! I'd toil and wait half a lifetime to call her my wife. See, she says:

"And white across the tide
The ship shall spread her snowy sail,
    To bring a joyous bride."

1113

CHAPTER XVII.

NARDO'S ADVENTURES.

AFTER the White Ship sailed away Nardo was depressed for a long time with melancholy; and, while cheered by the conversation with Melchisedec, still a year appeared long to an ardent and accepted lover. But after reading the hopeful and cheering lines from Rebecca - and he had discovered her resignation, philosophy, hope, and trust - he determined to so far control his temper, and strengthen his faith, and live such a life of purity, that the mirror would show no stain, and he would be worthy of the love of the matchless Rebecca. To accomplish this, he resolved to live the life of a hermit; to withdraw himself from the presence of man; to commune with nature; to dwell upon the goodness of God; to meditate upon the charms of his sweetheart. And the better to do that, he retired to a distant ridge of the mountains, which shut out the ocean, whose waters poured into the stupendous chasm already referred to in a former chapter.

Accordingly, he supplied himself with such provisions and implements as he needed, and in four weeks after Rebecca sailed away, with one attendant, named Iran, he took up his abode in a deep valley a hundred miles away. His tent was pitched under the side of a mighty cliff, where he spent his time. Behind the tent, and above on the side of the cliff, some thirty feet high, he hung his two hammocks, for himself and Iran, where they slept in perfect safety from prowling animals or evil-minded men. A rope-ladder ascended to the hammocks, and by lifting the rope and drawing it up, they felt no fear at night. The rock projected out over the hammocks so that no falling mist could reach them.

The tent was located on a rocky ledge, on each side of which flowed two streams of water, which united at the lower end, making thence but one stream. One was cold and clear and excellent to drink, and issued from a cave in the cliff; the other was a cold or hot stream, according to the hour. During the day it was cold and at night hot, and, while

SCENE OF NARDO'S ESCAPE.

A, Nardo's Fort. B, Rope Ladder. C, Hot Stream. D, Cold Stream. E, Platform. F, Cliff. G, Tunnel.

hot, the channel or cave in the cliff ran full with great noise and tumult.

As soon as he was comfortably fixed, Nardo, with a light, entered the dark tunnel of the cold stream to explore it. The water had cut a channel through the rocks about twenty feet wide and fifteen deep. He followed its winding course for half a mile, where it ended, and it came up through a deep, round pool, and rolling over the edge, formed the stream which flowed out near the tent and joined the larger stream some distance below. The next day, after the hot water subsided and the channel had time to cool, he explored the other stream. The channel was wider and higher, and he followed it about a mile, when he discovered an opening on the left, out of which the hot water evidently came, and fell some ten feet into the bed of the cool stream. The cave had been hot, and whenever the hand touched the rock it was seen that it was still quite warm. He followed the cool stream for a quarter of a mile, which rose rapidly, with little falls of three or four feet, and then the water gushed out of a hole ten feet square. Nardo seated himself upon a small projection on the rock and gazed upon the spouting fountain. Nearly all the way up he had waded in water to his knees, and feeling chilled, he wended his way back to the mouth of the hot stream, which was now dry; and clambering up, he explored it some distance, where he found another fall. In places were little pools of water, still warm, in which he bathed his hands and face, and this, with the warmth of the rocks, brought on a reaction, and soon he felt very comfortable. Having been a long time in the cave, he started back, exploring more leisurely. He clambered down the dry fall, and, stopping, examined matters more minutely. The moment he got down into the cold water he noted that the turn was square to the left, and if he had been pursued by the boiling stream, a sharp turn and traveling upwards would have saved him; but he was sure he had not overstayed his time. But he felt safest to be moving, and he leisurely started down the stream. When he had proceeded about two-thirds of the way his foot sunk into a water-hole, and falling, he went under, and his

THE HIDDEN WORLD

light was extinguished. When he arose again he was in a darkness so intense that it seemed to daze and stupefy him. It was so profoundly dark, he felt as if it could be gathered and put in his pocket. He was dazed for a time, and wiping his face and eyes, and while attempting to do the same to his hair, found his hat was gone. He stepped forward, feeling for his hat. His foot went into another hole, when he plunged under the water again. Alarmed to find so many holes, he struggled violently, regained his feet, and wiping his face, he stepped back, and down he went under the water again. This time when he regained his feet he was thoroughly frightened. Three times he had, in less than three seconds, stepped into three holes and been under the water. When he arose the third time he stood perfectly still for a time, afraid to step, and he had lost all idea of direction, and for his life he could not tell which was up, which down-stream, or which was across. As he ascended he had noticed that the stream was not generally more than twenty feet wide, and he had gone up on the right-hand side, where the water was seldom more than ankle-deep, and he knew nothing about the center or left side of the stream; and he now recollected that he had been returning on the other side, and that accounted for his mishap. Uncertain what to do, he hallooed, hoping Iran might hear him, but the sound was so terribly loud that it startled him. It was repeated many times, and came back loud and low, sometimes seeming near and loud; then as if some person had mocked him around a bend; then dodged out of the way, still mocking as they went, and then it appeared as if others had taken it up afar off.

These sounds were so uncanny that he hesitated to call for Iran a second time, knowing that he could not hear him, and after recovering his composure he felt down with his hands, and soon found deep water; he felt in the opposite direction, and finding no deep water there, then carefully felt around with his right foot, and continued to do so for some time; and after reflecting upon it he felt confident he must be going down stream, and so he turned to the right, taking step after step with more assurance, until he stepped into another water-hole and went under again.

1117

THE HIDDEN WORLD

He struggled quickly to regain his feet and found the water was over his head; he threw himself into a swimming position, arose to the surface, and swam with all his might, and after a few strokes his head struck a rock, and throwing up his hand he found he had probably reached the shore. He made a firm grasp when he ascertained he had indeed reached one or the other shore; he could not tell which way to go. He sat down on the stone, drew his feet out of the treacherous water, and felt like blessing the solid rock.

After resting and meditating for a while, he remembered with a start that he had been probably longer in the water and on the way than he should have been, and if night should come, he would be boiled in the torrent of hot water.

For a while this fear stupefied him. Then recovering all his fortitude and faculties, he concluded to put his hand into the water and see which way it was running.

But the current was so sluggish in the dark that he could not tell. Sometimes he thought it flowed one way, then the other, and then in a circle. Suddenly the thought came like a flash that he was so bewildered that he could not tell whether the water flowed against or from his hand. This alarmed him exceedingly. Could it be that he was losing his mind?

In this dire extremity he kneeled in the water, and keeping a firm grip on the rock, he spent a few fervent moments in prayer, and called upon Jeuss for help and guidance.

Suddenly, a greater confidence, peace, calmness, and even happiness pervaded his whole being, and something suggested that he "hold on to the shore, and travel, and don't delay," and he spoke aloud and said: "Jesus, be my guide! Lord, I trust all to Thee!"

He rose from his knees with perfect confidence, put his right hand on the shore, his feet in the water, and started. He had not gone far before he heard the flowing water, and soon he was in a riffle, and he knew to a certainty that he was going in the right direction. He then recalled the fact that he encountered such a riffle within three minutes' walk when he started up the stream. Greatly encouraged he pressed on with renewed courage and hope, and was con-

1118

THE HIDDEN WORLD

gratulating himself at his near approach to safety, when he heard a startling sound behind him; he listened for a second, and horror! the hot water was coming. The roar almost deafened him as it came thundering on, and he started to run and said:

"O Lord Jesus, save me!"

Simultaneous with the prayer, around an angle of the channel a light flashed, and Iran, his servant, was coming on a run towards him, holding a light above his head which illumined the cave as light as day. It flashed along the water, and Nardo ran through the stream to the other shore, up which he traveled, and shouted:

"Run, Iran, run back for your life, the hot water is coming."

Without an instant's hesitation Iran turned, holding the light above his head, and fled for his life, while Nardo, with a love for life, ran with all his speed, while the hissing water thundered after them. At this moment the glad light burst to view at a turn in the channel, and encouraged by the hope of safety, Nardo held his breath for a final burst for life, just in front of a wave of boiling, hissing water ten feet high. Iran easily escaped, and Nardo, on arriving at the rock on which his tent stood, leaped up, but he was too much exhausted to save himself; but Iran caught his hand and drew him up, and none too soon, for in a second after, the boiling, roaring torrent swept by, hissing as if angry at Nardo's escape. And the faithful Iran placed his panting master in a sitting position, and gazing at the impetuous torrent of boiling water, he said:

"Jesus be praised!" And turning to Iran, said, "Iran, bless your noble soul, you saved my life."

"Not me, kind master, it was he."

"He! Iran, whom do you mean?"

"Why, the venerable man with the white beard, who gave me the light, and said 'Run!'"

"What do you mean by light, Iran? Explain yourself."

"Well, do you see, I was wondering why you had not returned, and looking up, there he stood, beautiful, kind, with the light in his hand. He pointed into the cave and

1119

said, 'Go quickly.' I understood, took the light, ran with all my might, met you, and you escaped safely."

"The light! What light? Where is it, Iran?"

"Indeed, master, I don't know, it's gone; when I clambered up the rocks and turned to help you it disappeared."

Nardo seated himself, dropped his head upon his hands and sat a long time silent; then raising his head, gazed upon the impetuous torrent of hissing, boiling waters, and said:

"The sublime, wonderful power and protection of Jehovah, the mercy and goodness of Christ, the Old Man, the light, Iran, Rebecca - oh, Rebecca!"

CHAPTER XVIII.

TAMING PECCARIES.

THE adventure in the cave so far affected Nardo, that for several days he did not go away from his tent. During that time he directed Iran to do all he could to tame the birds and all harmless animals. The woods and valleys were full of animal life. Black and red squirrels and rabbits were plentiful, while birds sung and flitted everywhere. Wren, bluebird, robin, jay, pigeon, hawk, owl, pheasant and wild turkey abounded. Deer and bears were often seen. Neither Iran nor Nardo threw at them or scared them; they flew and wandered all around, and soon grew so accustomed to their presence that all was as merry as if men were not around. Pigeons in large flocks loaded the trees, pheasants drummed, squirrels ran up and down trees, jumped from limb to limb, and chattered and frisked from tree to tree and from bough to bough. The turkeys seemed the wildest, and at first the deer, bounding away and finding themselves not pursued, occasionally showed themselves and grew tamer day by day. They would let Iran or Nardo pass by without running, but they kept their eyes upon them vigilantly, and on the fourth day they saw a flock of peccaries some distance away, and Nardo said:

"Iran, they say that the peccaries are untamable. These peccaries have probably never seen a man; let us try what

1120

kindness and tact will accomplish with them. Fix our rope ladders where we can ascend high enough to be out of their reach, and you collect a large amount of peaches and plums, and when the peccaries come let us climb above their reach and feed them, and see if they will eat, or if they are untamable and irredeemably malicious."

So when the peccaries passed out of sight Iran collected a quantity of peaches and plums and placed them on a platform some twelve feet high, and prepared for the next herd of peccaries that should appear. Two days after they saw a flock approaching, and as soon as they heard Nardo and Iran talking, which they did, the peccaries halted, gathered in a bunch, tossed up their heads, looked ugly, and then, with rising bristles, advanced directly toward them, but Nardo and Iran continued to talk, and passed back and forth as if paying no attention to them, but carefully noting all their actions. When the peccaries arrived on the bank of the little cold-water stream, they halted, and shook their heads when Nardo said:

"I believe, Iran, they will cross, and perhaps attack us; keep a sharp eye on them, and if they do cross the water, mount the ladder, get on the platform, but don't make any aggressive action or appear to be afraid."

As the animals seemed aggressive and inclined to attack, Nardo and Iran carelessly drew near their respective ladders, and when the peccaries started with a rush and made for them, before they could come near enough to do any harm, each one was up the ladder. When the peccaries arrived they were out of reach, and they continued talking. The peccaries looked up amazed, and, seeing no motions to assail them, their bristles came down a little, and they seemed disconcerted and did not understand what those strange beings meant, who showed neither fear nor a purpose to attack them. The leader jumped up towards them two or three times, then stood still, shook his head, and gazed directly upwards.

Nardo leaned down and said, "Good-day, friends," and dropped a handful of peaches, and when the leader saw it, he jumped up, caught a peach, and bit it furiously; he seemed

1121

nonplussed; instead of an offensive matter there was a juicy peach in his mouth. He spit it out at first, but seemed surprised, and Nardo dropped another handful. They were caught, dropped, picked up, and chewed and swallowed. Handfuls were dropped by both men, and presently one, and then another, put down their heads, picked up peaches, and while chewing intently kept their eyes steadfastly on Nardo and Iran.

Nardo stooped over and said, "Friends, will you have some more?" and he and Iran threw down a handful apiece, and in a short time the peccaries were eating and hunting around for them, and when all were picked up they lifted their heads as if looking for more. Nardo said a second time, "Friends, have some more," and half a peck was thrown down, and they hunted them like a herd of swine, and this was continued until all the peaches were gone, when Nardo got off the platform and descended part way down, at which their bristles came up, and the old patriarch seemed to have a recurrence of his savageness.

Nardo stooped and said, "You should not distrust your friends," and threw down some plums. They kept their eyes on him for a short period, and then commenced on the plums. This was continued for half an hour, when Nardo climbed back on the platform and up and down the ladder, but all the time out of reach of danger, and then, by his direction, Iran did the same, taking his place, and after a long time the peccaries became less distrustful and looked only for food; they lost to a considerable extent their wild, ferocious appearance. After feeding them until their hunger was appeased, Nardo and Iran climbed to their hammocks and went to sleep, and when they awoke the peccaries were gone. Looking sharply around in all directions, and seeing the coast clear, they descended and saw no more of them that day. To provide against further danger to their tent and provisions, they built a stone wall around the tent too high for the peccaries to mount over in case of a sudden attack. Also they erected a safe platform on the other side of the cool stream, and Iran was provided with plums and peaches, ready for the next appearance of the peccaries. They migrated from place to place, and it was a week before they were seen approaching again in single file, led by the same old pugnacious peccary.

Iran hurried to and mounted the platform, while Nardo ascended his ladder, to try their new plan.

When the peccaries were near Iran, he arose and called: "Sou, sou!"

The peccaries stopped instantly at sight of Iran, drew up in a huddle, the hair and bristles came up, the leader champed his jaws, shook his head, his eyes shone with rage, and his aspect was ferocious. The platform, and a man standing on it, was something none of them had ever seen before, but the voice of Iran calling "Sou, sou," which had been called so often a week before, had evidently some effect, and when he said: "Friends, have something to eat, sou, sou, sou," and then tossed some peaches to the ground, the leader seemed to remember something, and he slowly advanced to the peaches, and keeping his eyes intently on Iran, lowered his head, took a peach in his mouth, and jerking up his head, he looked straight at Iran while he munched the peach. Continuing to call "sou," he threw handfuls down, and soon the whole flock were eating the peaches almost as fast as they fell. Iran stopped for a while, and when the peaches were picked up from the ground, the peccaries all looked up at him. It was a comical sight, a line of fierce, implacable, ferocious beasts, with their sharp snouts uplifted, and their small but keen eyes fastened on him. He noticed their sharp tusks, and understood how dangerous these active and fearless animals would be, with their alert and dauntless courage. He then threw some peaches and plums to the right, and no sooner did they strike the ground than the whole flock, except the leader, scampered after them. The old patriarch of the flock stood guard, and while the others were picking up the falling fruit, Iran tossed a handful to him; he dropped his head and ate them. Peaches and plums were thrown with the right hand to the flock, and with the left, one at a time, to the old peccary, and so thrown that he had to advance step by step, until he was directly under Iran, who stooped over the side, and gently

1123

tossed a peach at a time to him. He looked up a moment, as taking the measure and meaning of Iran, and then, as if reassured, he ate the peach without distrust. From this time, the peccary only watched for peaches and plums, and pounded upon them as fast as thrown on the ground.

Finally, Iran stooped over, and calling, "Sou, sou," held out a peach in his hand, and there was but four feet between the extended hand and the snout of the peccary, a distance which the active animal could have jumped, and with a side swipe of his sharp tusk, ripped Iran's arm open, and disabled him for life. But the beast was looking for food, not fight, and when the peaches and plums fell, they were eagerly devoured. Iran sat down on the platform, swung his feet back and forth, calling "sou," and soon all the peccaries were around, intently getting their share of the food, and showing no symptoms of hostility.

Nardo, from his elevated position, had noticed carefully all that passed, and descending to the tent, he advanced to the edge of the stream, and stopping at a point where the rocks rose four feet precipitate above the water, said:

"Iran, stop feeding awhile, and let me experiment on these fellows," and Nardo called aloud, "Sou, sou." Every peccary lifted its head instantly, the old patriarch looked towards Nardo, shook his head, commenced to stamp with one foot, to champ his jaws, and advanced with all the others in hostile array; but just before they reached the bank, Nardo threw some large peaches which went spinning towards them. The line of advancing animals stopped, looked at the rolling fruit, and hearing the words "sou, sou," and noting the regular fall of food, they broke ranks and commenced to eat. This was continued until their appetite was satisfied, and when the peccaries wandered leisurely away, Iran descended from his platform, and joined his master. Thus had intellect, diplomacy, instinct, and appetite kept down a collision, for once at least, between man and beast. In less than a month the peccaries were so tame, that Iran and Nardo could go anywhere they pleased without being attacked, and they often shook down plums and peaches for them.

One day Nardo resolved to enter the cave of the hot

THE HIDDEN WORLD

stream and explore it, as he was curious of learning more about the numerous holes in the bed of the stream, where he came so near perishing. He took Iran with him, and each carried a light, so that the expedition should be guarded against danger from that source.

Ascending above the riffle they soon encountered the place of his adventure. Leaving Iran on the right bank up which they had traveled, Nardo, with his light in one hand and a pole to sound the water in the other, waded into the stream, carefully sounding at every step. The water was clear, running with only a perceptible motion, and the two lights made the bottom clearly visible. He had nearly crossed the stream, and was within a few feet of the shore, when he saw deep water, and thrusting in his pole, he found no bottom; turning to the right he took a couple of steps where he could plainly see the bottom, then curved to the left, and soon saw deep water again. He then traveled around this deep water-hole, sounding as he went, and soon was clear around an irregular hole, about fifteen feet long and ten feet wide, and it was the only place where the water was above his waist. He waded up and down, back and forth, but this was the only hole, and the only deep water he could find.

One can imagine his surprise and chagrin. He had been certain that he had fallen in different holes, but now he saw that in an irregular water-hole, ten by fifteen feet, he had nearly lost his life. In many places it was so shallow that it would not reach to his waist or chin, and in the darkness and fright he had stumbled into it repeatedly, believing that each was a different hole, and that the stream was all cut up with pitfalls and man-traps.

When he came to the shore, Iran said:

"Well, master, did you find them all?"

Nardo hesitated for an answer and then replied:

"I found the exact spots into which I plunged; and now we will return."

On their way out Nardo reflected upon the ridiculousness of his floundering around in a little hole, but it taught him that a man in Cimmerian darkness, so total and profound, and bewildering, as he had encountered, could readily lose

1125

control of himself and his wits, and he resolved hereafter to be cool and self-possessed.

CHAPTER XIX.

PECCARIES AND PANTHER.

IN returning to camp, they heard a great commotion and noise out towards the platform, where Iran had fed the peccaries. These animals were jumping up and snapping their jaws, and lo! on the platform, was a large panther, with a dead peccary between his paws, tearing off the flesh and eating it, while the animals below were making a great noise, and frantic efforts to get at the panther. Now just above where their hammocks hung was a ledge of rocks which ran along the cliff, out and beyond and above the spot where the panther lay. One upon that ledge was beyond the spring of the animal, and Nardo and Iran quickly clambered on to the ledge and silently hastened to assist the peccaries, Nardo with spear, and Iran with bow and arrow, and they soon worked their way out silently, opposite and above the panther.

Notwithstanding the noise of the peccaries, the panther was stripping the flesh with his teeth, holding the dead peccary down with his paws. He was so busy eating that, with the noise of the animals, his human foes were not heard or discovered before they gained a favorable position.

By a concert of action Nardo hurled his spear, while Iran sent an arrow whizzing almost at the same instant.

The spear went through a paw of the panther, and fastened it to one of the round logs which made a part of the platform.

The arrow struck in the loins. When they threw and shot, Nardo and Iran shouted aloud. The panther attempted to spring to his feet, but finding one foot fast, he bit at the spear and pulled desperately to free his foot from the same, and, whirling around, his hind feet fell off the platform. He struggled desperately to regain his position. With one foot held by the spear he could not speedily regain the platform. The peccaries were jumping up and ripping his legs and flanks with their keen tusks.

But, making a supreme effort, the panther caught one hind foot on a pole, and attempted to rise, and he would have succeeded, had not the shank of Iran's arrow caught and held him down in spite of his frantic efforts. The strain could not last long. The log, where the panther's hind foot was clinched, turned, and with a spear in his foot, and an arrow through his flank, panther, spear, and arrow fell to the ground.

The beast struck upon his back. The peccaries pounced upon him in a bunch, and there was a terrible commotion of cries, howls, grunts, squeals, and snorts. Heads, heels, snouts, tails, ears, and bodies were mixed and mingled in inextricable confusion. The panther occasionally threw a peccary up in the air, but before he fell half a dozen took his place. Finally the foot was torn loose, and the panther for the first time regained his feet and attempted to mount a tree; but the peccaries covered him instantly, and it was not long before he was slain, and for more than half an hour they ripped and tore him. Thus he paid the penalty for his rashness in attacking and attempting to make a meal upon the most ferocious little brute that walks the earth.

It took more than a month to bring the peccaries back to the condition of tameness they were in before the fight with the panther.

CHAPTER XX.

IRAN'S REPORT - THE OLD MAN - NARDO'S RESOLVE AND JOURNEY.

SOME days after the last transaction, Iran came in from an extensive tour, and his appearance indicated some excitement, and as soon as he approached Nardo near enough to talk, he said, "I've seen him again, and he pointed out the way."

"Seen whom, and what way do you mean?"

"Why the Old Man, the one who handed me the light when I went into the cave to meet you; don't you remember?"

1127

THE HIDDEN WORLD

"Yes, I shall never forget you or the light; but tell me all about meeting the Old Man - all the details."

"Well, I was up yonder, after peaches and plums, when something made me look up, and there standing on the side of the precipice, away up on that dark rift or place we have so often seen and talked about, there stood the Old Man, and although so high up and far away, he seemed the same size as when he handed me the light. He didn't say anything to me then, but he pointed the way, and then I could see a place winding along the cliff and gradually ascending away up the ravine to where a tall tree is, and by climbing up on that tree one could go up to where the Old Man stood. He then pointed to the left, and I could see a pathway along the dark line we have seen, and with the light in his hand he walked along. The light showed the path till he got to the shoulder of the cliff yonder, when he stopped, and pointing around it he said:

" 'The path for your master.'

"He then went around out of sight, but I could see the gleam of the light for a while after he vanished out of sight. Then I remembered what he said, and I hastened to tell you."

"Well, Iran, you tell me a marvelous story; were it not for the light, the day you rescued me, and your seeing him that day, I should distrust all you say, and call it an illusion. I must say you could not hear him speak at such a great distance."

"I don't care what any one says; I saw him, I heard him speak, and I saw the light, and I know him and the light, and I would know it and him anywhere."

"It is all strange, Iran, but Melchisedec and myself saw an old man on a rock, when the river sunk and the terrible earthquake occurred, when we were on the outside of the world, and if it was that man, I would not be afraid to meet him anywhere."

"Meet him anywhere! afraid! I guess not. Why, he's the most peaceful, kind, gentle-hearted man I ever saw, and I was perfectly happy, and felt safe while looking at him. Safe! I guess it is."

"Well, Iran, get everything we need for a journey of

1128

three or four days. In the morning we will start. See about this road along the cliff, find where it leads to, and what comes of it. The light he gave you saved my life. We can trust him, and if we cannot trust him we can trust Jesus."

The next morning they went out into the valley, and scanned the face of the cliff. Away up at a dizzy height, they could discern a dark line which seemed to be a black trace running along the face of the cliff, extending away off to the right, gradually ascending the ravine where Iran said the tree was; but to the left the dark line trended upwards, until it reached the shoulder of the cliff, where it turned abruptly to the right, or ended, they could not tell which. It seemed a long distance away, and a dizzy feeling crept over them to look up so high.

An eagle was sailing along half way up. It looked like a dangerous undertaking to travel along such a stupendous height, and after considering it for some time, Nardo said:

"Iran, that's far in the air. We'll take plenty of ropes, tie ourselves together, try the thing, practice care, and be prudent in all matters, for you see, one misstep and we could be dashed to death far below."

"Yes, master, but the Old Man showed the way, and where he went will be safe. Besides, we will take our lights; they will light our way for us as his did for him."

"Well, Iran, if the Old Man was just as we are in all respects, what you say would be correct, but you will recollect that Melchisedec and myself saw him on a rock, where no mortal could get. He has appeared twice to you, as if he came out of the air; you have seen his light twice, both times in the daytime. These lights came and went at his wish; you must see that there is something mysterious in the light, in his appearance, and disappearance; but notwithstanding, I am still resolved to go and see what becomes of the matter."

Iran scratched his head, as if in a quandary, and then said:

"Yes, master, it does seem queer, but I'd trust the Old Man any way, and I'm ready to go."

Nardo smiled, and replied:

1129

"Well, Iran, you trust him. I'll depend on your fidelity; as for me I know who I trust, and I'll lean on the arm of One who is all-powerful, who will never desert the faithful and deserving, so it is settled that we go; but, Iran, remember that no obstacles in the way must daunt us, or make us turn back. If is is decreed for us to go, we will find protection in our sorest need."

"Master," said Iran, "where you go, and the Old Man points the way, I'll go, if the old Abaddon himself stands in the way."

And so, provided with ropes, lights, and provisions, after placing all things in a proper condition for their absence, the next morning, bright and early, they took their way up the valley, which gradually ascended as they proceeded.

Under Iran's lead, after going a couple of miles, they turned out into a lateral ravine running to the left, continued ascending at a steep grade for several miles, when another turn was made, a steeper ravine was encountered, up which they traveled and wearily climbed, until, turning an abrupt line of rocks to the right along which they had been traveling for the last half mile, they saw before them an abrupt cliff, and there, sure enough, was a tree standing, and two-thirds as high as the tree, in the perpendicular cliff, could be plainly seen a fissure, or opening in the rocks, evidently the bed of a stream long ages ago, when the rocks were nearer the surface of the earth, and before they had been displaced, in some great upheaval which had lifted them high in the air. On beholding this Nardo said:

"Well, Iran, there is the tree, and the dark line or ledge which seems to once have been the bed of an extinct stream, and if it is as broad all the way up as it is here, if we keep in the center, there will be no danger of falling off."

"No, indeed, master. Now you let me climb the tree, and draw up the rope ladder, and then you can come up readily."

"All right, Iran, do so."

Taking a string with him, Iran soon climbed the tree, and from an elevated bough he looked towards the cliff and

1130

THE HIDDEN WORLD

exclaimed:

"Why, master, it looks like the cave where the hot water flows, if one side was knocked off to let in the light. It's more than twenty feet wide, and if we walk in the bed we could not look down the side of the precipice."

Iran then unwound his string, and let it down, to which Nardo fastened a rope. Iran drew it up, and securely fastened it to a large limb of the tree which grew over and reached on to the ledge. Provisions, water, and all their accouterments were drawn up, and then Nardo ascended.

It was as Iran stated. The bed of the stream was now dry and smooth except where there were small falls four to six feet high, but they found no difficulty in surmounting them. Indeed if they had not often looked up and out at the left upon the light, they would not have known they were up at such a great altitude. After starting they went upwards at such a grade that the stream must have flown with great velocity, and every step took them higher.

At one place, where the parapet of rocks was but two feet high, they approached the edge and attempted to look down, but the distance was so immense that they drew back, faint; their heads grew dizzy, and it seemed that the channel of the dry stream they were following must surely fall in.

But the massive, solid appearance of the rocks reassured them, and they passed on. By noon they had arrived where the shoulder of the precipice turned to the right, where the cave went directly into the mountain, and it looked dark and gloomy within. Here they halted, and prepared to spend the rest of the day and the night. Iran was sent back for the things, including the candles, rope, and water, while Nardo selected a spot to encamp and sleep. At the elbow, where the channel entered the precipice, was a flat rock ten feet wide and thirty long, which had been above the water when flowing here. At this point Nardo determined to spend the night.

After Iran left, Nardo fastened a rope securely, and tying the other end to his waist, he mounted the low parapet which marked the original bank of the stream, and took a hasty look. It was a dizzy, but a grand spectacle. It was a

THE HIDDEN WORLD

half mile down to the place where his tent was located. He could not pluck up the courage to look over far enough to see it. A creepy sensation went over him. Instinctively he drew back, as the terrible chasm yawned beneath him. Birds were flying far below, and looking around the shoulder he saw a deep valley beyond the precipice which had always barred the way below from this point, and he saw a thunderstorm sweeping along a deep valley between two mountains. The storm was coming quarterly towards him, miles away, and much below the spot where he stood. The sky was clear above and below the storm-cloud. The cloud rolled along, the end whirling in a circle, and a sudden flash of lightning would blaze out, and a dense cloud of mist shoot in in front like a cannon discharging. The mist would spread out right and left - a report, then a crash and rumble of the thunder would be heard, and while all the air trembled the thunder would go rolling from peak to peak. In front the cloud discharged almost continuously, flashing and belching out like a cannon, and rolling and whirling mist out thirty to fifty feet, while the flanks rolled clear over the valley, reaching across from side to side. Immediately after each report raindrops instantly formed, each drop distinct from all the others, commenced to fall, and their entire course could be seen until they reached the ground. In the front flank of the advancing storm, the rocks and the trees could be seen partially obscured by the falling drops, and in the rear the thickening drops became so numerous, and the mist so thick, that the earth was shut out. Only a vast white sheet of mist could be seen, while the flashing lightning in its momentary glare illumined the misty sea, and the roar and boom of the thunder rolled majestically onward. The vanguard of the cloud, with its crash and roar, disappeared around a bend, nothing could be seen but the misty sea, while the roll and growl and distant boom of the thunder could be heard growing less and less, until it ceased altogether. After a time the misty sea dissolved, grew into vapor, the vapor disappeared, trees, and ground shone like diamonds, a scene of transcendent brightness and loveliness followed, until the drops of rain dissolved, and as suddenly

1132

THE HIDDEN WORLD

SCENE IN THE INNER WORLD.

disappeared.

In looking upon this scene, Nardo thought, "How beautiful, how grand, elusive, and what a type of the world's delusions! We look to where the mountain-tops and the sky meet, and they seem to blend and become one. We see the clouds, and the ocean touch far away; they seem to blend and become one, but it is a delusion. The sun seems to rise and set, but it shines forever.

"The stars appear to wax and wane, but they are there forever. My mind goes out towards creation, but it soon tires, and I have no comprehension of eternity. How silly is man to attempt to fathom God! As certain as the flashing lightning, the rolling thunder bring rain to refresh the earth, filling the springs, flushing the mountains, so surely does the Spirit of Christ come to the soul, his Comforter fill the Christian with a happiness indescribable, and I thank God that I can say 'that my Redeemer liveth.'

"Here, on this dizzy precipice, in the valley where the peccaries and panthers fight, along the valley where the thunder rolls, and the lightning flashes, He is found, He is everywhere, omnipresent and omnipotent."

In due season Iran returned, and after supper they lay down to rest, half a mile higher than ever before, but apparently no nearer the sailing moon, or the twinkling stars, though far above the mass of mankind, yet two thousand miles under the feet of men on the outside of the world we live in, and here we leave them for the night.

* * * * * * * * * * * * * * *

Because of the extreme length of this novel, the balance of it will be presented in the Fall, 1962 issue, Issue No. 7. This issue will be available within several weeks. If you miss your copy, they can be secured by writing to THE HIDDEN WORLD, Inner Light/Global Communications
PO Box 753
New Brunswick, NJ 08903
www.conspiracyjournal.com

THE HIDDEN WORLD

LETTERS

FROM THE READERS

Where pertinent information concerning The Shaver Mystery is solicited from those who may have facts of value to offer.

Dear Mr. Palmer,

It was a very melodious baritone voice, with just a touch of derision. It said:

"You're going to die in that bed."

I said: "No, I'm not."

"Yes, you are going to die in that bed," said the voice, clear and gleeful.

"O, no I'm not. I'm perfectly healthy. There's nothing the matter with me," I said.

"O, yes! You're going to die in that bed."

"I am not, and you're a liar," I snapped. Then I turned off the light and crawled into bed, and was soon asleep.

This conversation took place March 10, 1961, about 1:30 A.M. I had been on 20 hour duty as a practical nurse for 6 days, and had gone back to my room for a 24 hour day off. I'd done a little shopping, then went to my rooming house, to my room; written a few letters, read awhile, had my supper, read some more, and then went to bed about 10 o'clock.

I woke about 1:15, turned on the light, and went to the bathroom for a glass of water. Then I sat down on the bed to remove my slippers. And that's when the voice spoke.

It was a beautiful voice. Clear as a bell, and a rich baritone. It sounded like its owner might break into a laugh or a song at any moment, but with the tiniest hint of derision in it. The trouble was, it hadn't an owner.

There was no one but me in the room. The two other

1135

women who had rooms there were both out; as were the owners of the place, who lived downstairs. The only other occupant was their dog, locked in the basement.

Was it a Dero who had discovered me alone and tried to frighten me?

Or was it, as many think, an angel of the Father, sent to warn me of a coming illness?

I don't know, but I do know that the next week I was taken ill, had to leave my employment to go to my home. I spent 7 days in the hospital, and am just now able to go back to work. To tell the truth, I'm just a little afraid to go back and sleep in that bed. Wouldn't you be, too? - Mrs. Eunice Ryan, 139 N. Main St., Adams, Wisconsin.

● This sort of "voice in the night" is typical of what Mr. Shaver calls "ray talk". It should not be taken seriously in that it almost always is not truth. The intent is only to upset and disturb. This is a sadistic joke. It is "idle chatter". If the "dero" were to carry out his prediction by some use of a killing ray, he would almost certainly be the cause of his own death as some other dero or a tero caused his ray to recoil upon him. (At least, this is Mr. Shaver's explanation.) There is another explanation, in that the dero is so closely associated with his "victim" that he includes himself in whatever destruction he visits upon his victim. Some readers may make sense out of the word "obsession" in this case. But then, what is "obsession"? It is an interesting question, which will, in a future issue, take on new meaning to those who are willing to think about the things we will present in the future on just this subject of voices that are heard in the night. - Rap.

Dear Ray,

This happened about 12 or 13 years ago. I was in my late teens, I think, but perhaps the time is not as important as the incident.

In the late night hours I awoke, got out of bed, walked out of the house and was met by a group of men (?) who drove me out into the country to an old farmhouse. I don't know the location anymore than the people involved; maybe

I was drugged, I don't know. At the farmhouse we went immediately to the potato cellar and through a trapdoor in the floor down a long inclining tunnel. We arrived into a room, fantastically decorated, bizzare, like Hades - how can I describe it? It was of good size; and others were present. Some one asked: "Is he ready?" and the answer: "Yes, he is." Two "others" - one on each side of me escorted me into a room? Tunnel? (again beyond my description) the worm, or whoever or whatever he or it was, was huge, long, round, knobby. An immense head and mouth (which swayed back and forth) spoke to me. I don't remember what it said or my answer, but one of them put a syringe into it, and then into me! I swear the language spoken by them and myself was not English, but something I seemed to know, yet but not know. After some kind of warning and benediction from this being, I was escorted out. Once again the car, the return trip, and home in bed. Since that time I have once in awhile visited the caves quite unhindered through my psychic senses, in dreams and the like. I can only comment that the knowledge of, and use of the mechs, the architecture, the philosophies in the pictures (or whatever they are), would enable man to live like gods in comparison to how they now live. However the areas of horror beyond comprehension would have to be removed before this can be.

An interesting sequel to this (dream or reality?) is that I have prayed, hard, that this wouldn't affect my life. I believe in some ways it hasn't, but my wife feels that something, as I also have felt, is not allowing me to live as I want to. Of course I want to know, was it dream or reality? (Name deleted by request.)

● Here we have a very interesting "dream". The reader will find some surprising parallels to material in Shaver's very first stories. Your editor believes them to be fantasies created by those mysterious entities Shaver calls the "dream makers". - Rap.

Dear Ray:
    I have just completed reading the Spring edition of the

1137

"Hidden World" and for the first time the complete story of the Shaver Mystery.

As a subscriber to both Flying Saucers and Search I have been excited and stimulated beyond description in reading many of your editorials and letter to editor replies. However, after reading about Shaver my body and mind feel like an exploding volcano. I'm so excited and my mind so full and my imagination soaring that I will not attempt to express in words what I feel. I know that you know.

I will learn this Mantong alphabet and dictionary and add to it when possible to help me understand more fully and seek out the truth. However, I do not want to use this only to enjoy my idle nights. How can I be instrumental in helping the Tero and our Earth people to gain insight into this "Hidden World" and seek out its positive assets to change the present course of humanity? In what manner can I help through the physical assets of my body and mind? What is needed?

Will you put me in touch with Shaver either directly or through this letter? Can I expect to hear from him? I am making a serious attempt to take an active role. - Murray Davidson, 70 Sedgewick Avenue, Yonkers, New York.

● Mr. Shaver lives at Rt. 2, Amherst, Wisconsin. He will be happy to receive letters from anyone who cares to write to him. - Rap.

Dear Mr. Palmer:

Why do you continue pretending that Richard Shaver exists? If he really does exist, where is a picture of him, a life-history, his present address, etc?

Of course it is a convenient fiction. You can make outrageous theories and claims without seeming to be making them youself. You can produce an entertaining series of sexy and adventuresome stories which appeal to the mythical-minded. You can earn your living. You can make potato pancakes on Saturday nights. You can invent "Dottie", "Jim Wentworth", "John Carson Buford", and all the others you need in order to have them say and do as you please to

1138

seem to have all kinds of legitimate "verification" of your own story.

I have rather closely analyzed yours and Shaver's writing and find too many similarities to deny this allegation, which claims that Ray Palmer is Richard Sharpe Shaver and a host of lesser deities in the menagerie. You are faking.

However, I hope you continue "faking", for if, as I suspect, you have included a hidden confession and explanation for your wild stories, this confession is the justification for your work of huge imagining. In the Spring 1961 issue of Hidden World you wrote: (you admit it) "... Tens of thousands of men and women have testified that the Shaver Mystery has changed their lives, opened up vistas undreamed, furnished them with valuable tools to enhance and make more purposeful and hopeful the grim business of living."

Please keep the Shaver yarn going! It's good fun, Mr. Palmer! - Bob Carricaburu, Winthrop J-23, Cambridge 38, Mass.

● This is the kind of letter we like to receive! It offers us such a wonderful opportunity to confound. If Mr. Carricaburu were to visit Amherst and be confronted with Mr. Shaver AND Ray Palmer, the expression on his face would be interesting to observe. But he does have a point - we will, in the next issue, present a picture of both Mr. Shaver and Ray Palmer, plus Shaver's life history (we have just given his present address), and anything else that may be of interest to Mr. Carricaburu and our other readers. If there is any need to convince himself, Mr. Carricaburu can check the police files of Chicago to learn the reality of Mr. Buford and his suicide. Any personage mentioned in the Shaver Mystery can readily be proved to exist - however, it is not our position to accept such challenges as this; it would waste too much of our time. Anyone who wants to back us down need only get up off his lazy backside and investigate - and then tell our readers he did so, and found our claims to be accurate. As to the similarities in the writing of Shaver and Palmer, this is true for the simple reason that every word written by Shaver has

1139

THE HIDDEN WORLD

been "edited" by Ray Palmer. Shaver admits to no great ability with the written word. His style is not of the best. For better reading quality, who can object to literary improvement by Ray Palmer, as long as the facts remain unchanged? - Rap.

Dear Mr. Palmer:

I have hesitated for some time to write this letter, however, since reading your last paragraph on Page 956 of the "Hidden World", I have decided that the following item would be of some interest to both you and the readers of the "Hidden World". The incident to which I am referring in the following occurred at approximately the time between the first and second issue of the "Hidden World". After reading the first or second issue, I forget which, this incident did happen in n.y office.

A patient came to my office whom I had treated approximately 3 years prior to that date. This patient had suddenly quit and disappeared. I could find no reason at the time for this patient stopping her treatments. At the time she was under treatment she was having some family trouble, namely with her husband. They were verging on divorce; she also had quite poor health and was quite upset. This woman was a woman of approximately 50 years of age. In spite of the fact that this woman was in poor health physically she checked out as an average mentally balanced person for her years and I'm quite positive there was nothing wrong with her from a psychiatric standpoint. So much for the groundwork of this woman.

Now, after approximately 3 years of absence, she told me that she came in to have a treatment and she wished to tell me something regarding the time lapse between stopping her treatments and the present time, thinking that I may be interested in knowing the outcome of her case. Therefore, I sat and listened to the following story. She said that at the time she quit treatment she did so because of the upset in the family and the pressure that was brought to bear upon her from many aspects. She had separated from her husband and had possession of their home. She stated he

1140

had moved out shortly before she was taken from the home. The method in which she described her removal was quite phenomenal. She said that she had noticed peculiar feelings over her body at various times for days prior to the initial removal. She also noticed that she had been observed around the neighborhood from cars and by people walking by, and at the moment that she was taken from the house she was sitting in the living room in a chair when the front door opened without any ring or knock; a man stood in the door and pointed his finger at her and she became immediately paralyzed from the waist down, unable to move a muscle. The man advanced 3 or 4 feet into the room and another man came through the front door beside him and stood and looked at her and suddenly her arms were pinned to her side, and merely by the man pointing across the room she was left speechless and unable to move her arms or her legs; she was totally paralyzed, frozen in the chair. They came over to her and handcuffed her and put cuffs also around the ankles so that she could not possibly get away. As soon as the cuffs were placed upon her, the feeling came back into her body and she regained her voice. Upon her inquiry, as to the reason for all of this, they told her that she was insane and that they would have to remove her to ------hospital. (------ hospital is a hospital for the treatment of psychiatric disorders). She was conveyed to ------ in a truck with 4 men being present, one of them purporting to be a doctor. Upon admission to ------, she described the various treatments which were given to her. These treatments consisted of hypodermic injections to increase the sexual libido in her and also they told her that these were an experiment and they were good for her and would help to get her well. Being a normal woman sexually and mentally, she resisted all the impulses which she was subjected to, both hypodermically and verbal suggestions. They also gave her pills to take which she was told would help to get her well but they admitted they were experimental pills and as she said they did everything to make her feel that she was mentally imbalanced and insane and that she must increase her sexual libido. From the

1141

time which she left the house and arrived at ------ she admitted and said that she heard voices; voices which would come out of chairs, out of the wall or would arrive in her head from no apparent source, whatsoever. The type of conversation, or the type of statements which came to her, such as I previously stated, were in actual description similar and almost identical to many of the voices of head and mental sayings described by Shaver in the first and second "Hidden World". At this junction of her story, I stopped her and called my nurse and my son, Dr. Earl Black into the room and told them I wished them to listen to the story for verification, whereupon I asked this patient the following questions: Are you a religious person, to which she answered, "no more than the average person I would term and no less. I occasionally go to church and enjoy it but I am possibly not as religious a person as I should be". Next question was, have you ever read any occult or metaphysical or spiritual books of any kind, upon which she said "no, I never have. I don't even know what you're talking about". The next question, have you ever heard of or read a magazine called "Search" magazine or "Fate" or have you by an coincidence read or heard of the "Hidden World" or any of the writings or quotations about the writings of the "Hidden World "upon which she answered "no, she did not know what I was talking about." And finally, have you ever heard of the Shaver Mystery? She replied "no". After determining these facts, I asked her to go back and repeat the story up to this point, which she did accurately and told me that even now and since that time she still has voices in her head which she could hear without bothering her and she normally resisted a lot of their foolish statements; some of them would be urgings to get up and slap someone in the face or to insult them verbally or to say obscene, vulgar phrases to them and in some instances to take a knife or something and attempt to assault a person. These statements she said she had learned to live with and to resist them totally as she did from the very beginning. She apparently had no knowledge of where they came from, did not become excited about

1142

them and knew within her own mind that this was coming from elsewhere other than her own personality or her own physical forces, and seemed to maintain a very calm equilibrium and approach to the entire matter. She went on to say that after several months, almost a year of confinement in ------ hospital with experimental treatment of such fantastic happenings that I cannot even relate on these pages, that a friend and lawyer finally obtained her release. After her release, she was invited to go to New Mexico and live with a friend to recover from her shocking experiences in ------ hospital. She had moved to New Mexico and had been living there all of the time since leaving the hospital until coming back at this time to California for a visit with friends at which time she came to see me. She described having heard these voices no matter where she was after she left during the 2 or 3 year period, and that occasionally she became quite perturbed about them, but she did not become excited about them. One aspect of the things which she said dealt with the political, economic information which was given to her from these sources concerning our country and our people, our government and the actual chaos which it is actually in to a degree of which we all know it is. We also know that there are forces working against the constitutional set- up of this country of which much information was given to her along this line. However, being a person not politically inclined nor a great intellectual endowed person she did not have the access to any of this information from any other source and cared nothing about the actual politics or economics because she, a mother, grandmother and a housewife had never become involved in governmental or economic and political facets of this country. I might add that I could in no way find any connection between her and any organization of any kind or even prove that she had ever read anything pertaining to things in the psychic realm. After listening to her story, I thought immediately of the first issue and revelations within the "Hidden World", because many of the experiences and statements which she told about were almost identical with many which Mr.

1143

Shaver described happened to him in the beginning of the Shaver mystery. This woman also responded normally in every manner to an interrogation which would reveal a mental flaw in the average person. Her response was completely normal; she was a well-balanced individual. While giving this patient her treatment, I decided to experiment with controlling the voices and statements which were coming through to her head. I wished to find out whether it were possible through treatment or outside influence by an experienced person or doctor if those voices could be stopped or influenced in any manner whatsoever. Through a method I have used for years connected with the psychic forces in 15 minutes time I was able to block out all of the voices completely which she was hearing so that they could no longer come through. However, after 15 to 30 minutes time following the treatment they were coming back in a milder manner. Whether the mildness persisted or whether she came back to full force in hearing the voices later, I do not know. I plan to contact this woman again soon to see how she is getting along. If I find anything of further interest in this case I will inform you. If you should publish this, please delete the name of the hospital for I don't think they would appreciate that type of publicity. - Paul L. Black, D.C., 725 South Long Beach Boulevard, Compton, Calif.

● This is a very significant and important letter. It is only one of hundreds we have received giving almost identical information. In it we find the real evidence of the "secret government" talked about by many sources. We find a belief in it in occult circles, in Shaver's material, in political factions, in religious groups, in the most unusual places and persons. This politcal angle is particularly interesting, and the thought that our national and world politics may be under the influence of insane "dero" is a ghastly and frightening one. Yet it is one of the prime factors in many letters, and in many experiences through the years since 1943 which has impressed this editor. That there is a basic truth in it there can be no doubt. In future issues we intend to present many items of information to corroborate this, and they will be items that can be confirmed. It is also disturbing to know as a fact that perfectly sane people can be and are being forcibly railroaded into insane asylums and experimented upon by drugs and various instruments, and even sexually degraded in unmentionable ways by persons we can only believe to be something unhuman or grossly degenerate. If it should be YOU who is thus railroaded, it would be quite important, would it not? But since it is not you, you will close your eyes to the facts concerning mental hospitals? A recent article in The Reader's Digest confirms this fact that many sane are illegally incarcerated in mental institutions. Today there is a Federal law on the books that makes precisely such kidnappings possible, without due recourse to law or jury trial. For those who question this, we invite them to look into the matter. Americans do not know what the mental laws of this country really say. - Rap.

Dear Mr. Palmer,

For about three weeks during June & July of 1960 I heard voices. I have never heard voices before or after this one episode. I have the same kind of life now as I had then; I mean I was under no unusual strain. I had two emotional shocks - the first a month before, the second, three days before the voices. It's hard to believe they were severe enough to make me go insane as they had no serious effect on me at the time.

I am almost convinced I was completely insane. The doubt comes from three incidents which involved other people. I picked apart two of them, but the third I can't - and I tried to in every way. I prefer a brief period of insanity over a hostile occult experience. It makes fascinating reading when it happens to other people, it's different when it happens to you.

I discovered occult science about two years before and spent quite a bit of time studying the subject. I discussed it with my husband and in his opinion it was a "lot of nonsense". He is a down-to-earth type, extremely critical (was) of anything which deviates from common knowledge.

The third incident happened during the last days of the

THE HIDDEN WORLD

voices and my husband was a witness. Afterwards, we went over everything very carefully and there was just no logical explanation. He now believes there are "things going on that most people don't know about". He even kidded me, a bit uneasily, about my poltergiest.

I have never told anyone about the voices, not even my husband. I first heard them when I was in the bathtub. One second everything was as it always was, the next second, I was insane. The voice seemed to come from within my mind and to be a distinct personality separate from me. It's hard to explain, but I was aware of a foreign presence, someone other than my own being. When these voices left me abruptly about three weeks later I was conscious of an emptiness in my mind, as though something had actually left it.

There were four or five of these entities and they took turns talking to me. I always knew when there was a change, even before they told me, as each had a distinct personality.

After a time, I managed to put this, more or less, out of my mind. I've always wanted an explanation but I didn't know where to go for it. I was cured a long time ago of talking about anything occult to my friends. I came across your magazine and several others by accident at the bookstore; I didn't know such magazines existed. The August, 1961 issue was the first Search I read and your editorial gave me quite a start.

The voices brought up many times what they called the "good influence" and the "evil influence", and gave them about the same meaning you gave the "invisible forces" you talked of in your editorial. In my occult studies I can't remember ever reading about such forces as described by you and the voices; only the powers a strongly developed human mind could exert.

The article by Afred W. Pritchard in the same issue reminded me of a conversation with one of the voices; (these voices would break in on my thoughts and say it was now time for another "lesson" or "truth"). The voice said the evil influence had taken over 60 percent of America, that it had infiltrated our government, and controlled our

THE HIDDEN WORLD

newspapers. I immediately thought of communists but the voice said that was not exactly what he meant. I asked about my newspaper but the voice said it was not important for me to know any more as the good influence would eventually win over the bad influence.

The more I write the more ridiculous it all sounds. Would you be interested in having me write out this experience in detail for possible publication? To me, it doesn't seem like anything you could publish; however, I would stake my life that the one incident which involved my husband was an occult experience.

My only interest in having this published is information. I am sure there must be someone among your readers who could explain what happened.

I must remain anonymous. If you haven't the time or facilities (or policy) to forward mail to me I wouldn't want to write out this thing.

Some of the letters you printed about others hearing voices was certainly a comfort to me. It made me feel better to know I'm not the only one. I admire the courage of these people for signing their names.

● We would certainly be pleased if you would tell us your whole story, and you can be sure the information will be as confidential as this letter. The details are important, because we can dovetail them with other reports. The fact that there are hundreds of identical experiences is proof of many things - reality, the fact this is not insanity, even temporary insanity as you call it, and that there does exist a "secret" power or "government", plus the realities behind the so-called "occult". The word occult means unknown. There is nothing weird about it. Once brought out into the open, it becomes knowledge, not occultism (a misnomer if there ever was one). - Rap.

(Editor's note: Letters are very important. For one thing they prove that the "Shaver phenomena" are still occuring, and for another, we need more facts. Whether you sign your name or not, let us hear from you, so that your experience can be published and add to the evidence we need to ferret out the HIDDEN WORLD about which this magazine is so

1147

vitally concerned. This issue of THE HIDDEN WORLD has suffered amazing reverses, but it has come out just the same. We are doing our part, against great difficulties; do your share by telling us your experiences. - Editor).

HERE NOW ARE the first TWO VOLUMES in a continuing series originally released by Publisher Ray Palmer in the 1960s, and hereby reprinted for the Serious Student of the Shaver and Inner Earth Mysteries!

**TO COME IN TOTAL 16 BOOKS, OVER 3200 PAGES AND ALMOST TWO MILLION WORDS!
14 MORE VOLUMES TO COME!**

HIDDEN WORLD NUMBER ONE:
The Dero! The Tero! And The Battle For Good And Evil Underground!

Here, in over 200 pages, is the beginning of The Shaver Mystery!

· Shaver hears the tormented voices coming from below.

· Readers question his sanity when he describes entering the caves of the ancients.

· He describes in detail the plunder of our planet by extraterrestrials in ancient times, and the lost continents of Lemuria and Atlantis.

· Shaver "proves his case" by revealing an ancient alphabet he calls "Mantong."

· Captured by the Dero from ancient races, the stem and mech machines cause utter chaos on surface dwellers, Wars, murder and horrific accidents are caused by the "evil ones."

THIS RARE REPRINT ONLY $25.00

HIDDEN WORLD NUMBER TWO:
The Masked World of Richard Shaver

The epic underground saga continues in roughly 190 pages of the nightmarish dealings with Inner Earth dwellers.

· A dark cloud hangs over the Earth as the subsurface mutants kidnap and torture humans, even performing cannibalistic acts upon their flesh.

· A series of airplane crashes carrying well-known celebrities can be blamed on the demented robot-like Dero.

· Shave reveals the secrets of "Growing A Better Man."

· Voices in the night torment readers of Shaver's tales as they confirm many of his claims.

THIS RARE REPRINT ONLY $25.00

SPECIAL OFFER: Both volumes One and Two of THE HIDDEN WORLD for the combined price of just $39.95. Please add $5.00 S/H to the total order.

Explore The Shaver and Inner Earth Mysteries

**Global Communications
Box 753 · New Brunswick, NJ 08903**

Free DVD On Inner Earth When You Purchase Any Three Items From This Advertisement.

RESEARCH AND BOOKS ON THE INNER EARTH, HOLLOW GLOBE AND SHAVER MYSTERIES

❏ The Smokey God and Other Inner Earth Mysteries—A voyage inside the earth and the truth about UFOs from Inner Earth and Telos, by Olaf Johnson, with Ray Palmer and Shurula—$15.00

❏ Etidorpha—Journet to Another Land. "Official Edition." 150-year-old classic. Secret Society member enters a cave in Kentucky to begin his strange journey—$25.00

❏ Subterranean Worlds Inside Earth by Timothy Green Beckley. Explores the Shaver Mystery and unexplained subterranean world tales—$15.00

❏ Richard Shaver and the Reality of The Inner Earth by Tim Swartz. Previous unpublished works with free audio CD—$25.00

❏ The Secret World—Rare hardcover classic with Ray Palmer and Richard Shaver, featuring his "rock book" paintings, with audio interview of Shaver and Palmer—$32.00

❏ Messages From The Hollow Earth by Dianne Robbins. Masters of Telos speak—$20.00

❏ Telos: The Call Goes Out From The Hollow Earth and the Underground Cities by Dianne Robbins—$18.95

❏ The Phantom of the Poles by William Reed— A rare classic long sought by collectors—$18.00

❏ Lost Worlds and Underground Mysteries of the Far East by M. Paul Dare—$18.00

❏ The Arctic Home in the Vedas by Lokomanya Bai Gangadhar Tilak. Rare Indian manuscript describes Inner Earth—$23.95

❏ Quest For Inner Earth by Dorothy Leon—$17.95

❏ Twilight: Hidden Chambers Beneath The Earth by T. Lobsang Rampa—$22.00

❏ Dweller On Two Planets by Philos The Tibetan. Early Mt. Shasta contacts—$19.95

❏ Incredible Cities of Inner Earth by David H. Lewis. Written in stunning, novel-like form, but all too true!—$21.95

❏ Mysteries of the Pyramid by David H. Lewis. Secret chambers revealed—$21.95

❏ Admiral Byrd's Secret Journal Beyond The Poles by Tim Swartz. Here is the untold, inside story, of a vayage beyond belief!—$22.00

❏ Caverns, Cauldrons, and Concealed Creatures, Expanded 2nd Edition! by Mike Mott. Thick book with color plates. Subsurface myths, legends and reality—$29.95

❏ Finding Lost Atlantis Inside The Hollow Earth. Rare reprint by Brinsley Le Por Trench. British Royalty gives excellent references—$22.00

❏ Missing Diary of Admiral Richard E. Byrd. Rare text, lost for years, now as a reprint—$15.00

Please add $5.00 for each book or every two books for S/H

**Global Communications · Box 753-TGS
New Brunswick, NJ 08903**

Credit card customers use our secure 24-hour hotline at 732-602-3407 — All major cards.
PayPal at MrUFO8@hotmail.com

www.ingramcontent.com/pod-product-compliance
Lightning Source LLC
Chambersburg PA
CBHW081225170426
43198CB00017B/2709